DECISION TRAPS

Ten Barriers to
Brilliant
Decision-Making
and How to
Overcome Them

J. Edward Russo
and
Paul J. H. Schoemaker

A Fireside Book
Published by Simon & Schuster
NEW YORK * LONDON * TORONTO * SYDNEY * TOKYO * SINGAPORE

FIRESIDE

Rockefeller Center
1230 Avenue of the Americas
New York, New York 10020

First Fireside Edition October 1990
Published by arrangement with Bantam/ Doubleday/ Dell Publishing
Group, Inc.
666 Fifth Avenue, New York, NY, 10103

17   18   19

Library of Congress Cataloging in Publication Data

Russo, J. Edward.
    Decision traps : the ten barriers to brilliant decision-making and how
to overcome them / J. Edward Russo and Paul J. H. Schoemaker.—A
Fireside ed.
        p.   cm.
    Reprint. Originally published: New York : Doubleday / Currency,
1989
    "A Fireside book."
    Includes bibliographical references and indexes.
    1. Decision-making.   I. Schoemaker, Paul J. H.   II. Title.
HD30.23.R87   1990
658.4'03—dc20
                                                    90-37506
                                                       CIP

ISBN 0-671-72609-9

To
Daniel Kahneman
Herbert Simon
Amos Tversky

whose path-breaking research provided
the intellectual foundation from which
our bridge to practice was built

Contents

DECISION TRAPS

Acknowledgments

We are pleased to recognize the special contributions of a few—among many others—who have made this book possible.

Colleagues. Much appreciated academic feedback was received from our friends and colleagues John Carroll (MIT), Josh Klayman (Chicago), Howard Kunreuther (Wharton), and Richard Thaler (Cornell).

Executives. Over a thousand managers have heard us lecture on the topics of this book. We especially wish to thank those executives whose support and interest made these many seminars fertile learning opportunities for all concerned: William Battle (Fieldcrest Mills), Ron van Beaumont (Royal Dutch/Shell), Garry Billings (Interpublic), Tom Broadus (T. Rowe Price), Richard Caldwell (Harris Bank), Jeff Diermeier (First Chicago), John Kirscher (Harris Bank), Lewis Lawton (Eastmet), Ed Mathias (T. Rowe Price), Vivian McCann (IBM), Nanty Meyer (University of North Carolina), Chuck Ransbottom (IBM), and Jack Rivkin (Shearson-Lehman).

Students. Numerous MBA students have provided us with helpful comments, insightful examples, and specific research projects. We especially wish to thank here Jim Andreanos, Beth Bader, Frank Bozich, Mary Anne Glunz, William Gurtin, Lloyd Nelson, Michael Sauer, George Searles, Harold Stuhl, Daryl Wikstrom, and Antonie Zoomers.

Assistants. We have received excellent administrative assistance from the business schools of both the University of Chicago and Cornell University. Special mention should be made of Pat Combs, Mary Lou Steger, Carol Signore, and Allison Wade for their secretarial support.

Editors. Earlier drafts of our manuscript received helpful editorial advice from Larry Arbeiter, John Brockman (our agent), Michael Fitzgerald, Jaine Mehring, Harriet Rubin and Janet Coleman (both from Doubleday). We are also grateful to Sarah Wernick (free-lance writer) for her assistance on the book's structure and style.

A special debt is owed to Robert Chapman Wood, who as our writer, reshaped the manuscript in the final few months to improve its accessibility and relevance to the reader. He performed admirably under constant deadline pressure, and we deeply appreciate his professionalism.

Lastly, we thank our families for their understanding and support, especially when the book started to encroach seriously on evenings and weekends. Joyce Schoemaker is in addition acknowledged for her critical readings of various drafts and her excellent suggestions.

Introduction
Decision-Making In the Real World

Good coaches help people realize their full potential. Sports coaches know the natural mistakes of untrained athletes and smart strategies for playing the game. They focus on a few key points—often simple points. Once you master these points, your play improves enormously.

Most people appreciate the value of good coaching. And most people, especially professionals, know that making decisions is the most important and transforming activity of their lives.

Yet few people have ever had any systematic coaching in how to make decisions. Most people, in fact, are almost completely self-trained in decision-making.

Over the past ten years, we've tried to change that. Our seminars teach excellent decision-making much as athletic coaches teach sports: by explaining the ways in which typical decision-makers err. We teach ways to avoid these mistakes, and show how people can master the decision process.

Why Does Decision Coaching Work?

We've been able to do this because of path-breaking academic research over the past twenty years by scholars such as Daniel Kahneman and Amos Tversky, and earlier work on how people process information by Herbert Simon, the 1978 Nobel Prize laureate in economics.*

These researchers have for the first time taken a detailed look at how real people make real decisions. This means analyzing the decision-making process much as a swimming coach analyzes each action of a swimmer's stroke, dive, or turn.

Good swimming coaches recognize that untrained swimmers tend to make a few characteristic errors such as diving in too deeply or raising their heads too high when they breathe. Researchers in decision-making have learned that untrained decision-makers make equally characteristic errors. For instance, people frequently define their problems in ways that cause them to overlook the best options. Or they fail to collect key factual information because they have too much confidence in their judgments. Just as the best swimming coaches have developed ways to overcome the most common errors of swimmers, decision-making researchers are developing ways to overcome the characteristic errors of self-taught decision-makers.

This is a truly new development. Traditionally, decision theorists had mostly asked themselves how decisions *should* ideally be made. Then they created mathematical models for people to follow. Unfortunately, those who applied their theories found the real world so complex that the models rarely helped much.

The innovative studies of the last two decades have faced up to the enormous complexity of the real world. They have examined how excellent thinkers cope with that complexity and how ordinary people can become excellent decision makers.

*Extensive Chapter Notes begin on page 229 to elaborate the basic ideas of each chapter, provide background information, and suggest additional reading, including many original sources.

These new decision researchers call their approach "behavioral decision theory" because it results from looking at how decision-makers actually behave. Numerous academic articles have made their striking insights freely available to other scholars, but until now this important work has never been readily accessible to the general reader.

We know from our coaching experience that these discoveries offer enormous value for ordinary business people. Indeed, they can help virtually anyone who makes decisions. Top corporate managers, lawyers, financial analysts, advertising executives, and physicians—people who share little more than the burden of making decisions—have told us that our coaching, based on these discoveries, has dramatically improved their lives.

Here are some examples:

Executives of a top advertising agency told us they were overwhelmed by cost pressures because clients were demanding lower commission rates. We urged them to state the problem in a new way. They needed to ask: How do other kinds of businesses cut costs without reducing perceived quality? In what ways is an advertising agency like a McDonald's restaurant or a university? Based on this type of thinking (which we'll show you how to do in Chapter 3), they started to curtail the unprofitable services they offered to clients (analogous to McDonald's offering a limited menu). They introduced efficiency measures based on careful analyses of the actual costs of various services. They rethought the pricing of services, introducing lower prices for a slow "off season" (such as a period between new car models for an agency specializing in automotive clients). By reframing their view of the business, they achieved major steps back toward prosperity.

An executive's two-year-old daughter was born with a hip defect. He was frustrated and confused after three different doctors advised three different treatments: One urged a major operation, another a rigid brace, and a third advised waiting for six more months. We helped the father "frame" his choice: We advised him to ask the doctors to separate their scientific opinions from their personal values. Doctors' scientific opinions represent their medical expertise, and merit deep respect. Doctors' personal values are no better than anyone else's. Did the two doctors opposing the operation really expect a result different from the doctor who favored it? "No," they said. However, they did fear that the long period of recuperation would disrupt the social development of a two-year-old. Now the father could weigh the alternatives rationally. He knew that his wife and five other children could travel to the city where the operation and rehabilitation would be performed. They could provide plenty of social support for the immobilized daughter. He okayed the operation. It worked beautifully.

A former MBA student, Jay Freedman, is a top analyst at the investment firm Kidder, Peabody and Company and credits our teaching for having contributed directly to his "best investment advice." Within six years of leaving the University of Chicago he was ranked the Number 2 household products analyst in America by *Institutional Investor* magazine. He says he learned from us how to overcome the normal human tendency to be overconfident in personal judgment. For instance, when gathering intelligence on a company he deliberately asks questions designed to "disconfirm" what he thinks is true. If Freedman thinks the disposable diaper business is becoming less price competitive, for example, he will ask executives a question that implies the opposite such as, "Is it true that price competition is getting tougher in disposable diapers?" This kind of question makes him more likely than competing analysts to get the real story, and Freedman's "buy" recommendations have consistently added value for his clients. (One of us remembers well his unusual recommendation to buy Unilever at $88 in 1984, when this European company was little known to U.S. investors. On a split-adjusted basis it was trading at over $300 per share in 1989.)

We shall mention other successes throughout this book. The point, however, is not that we think we are brilliant coaches. It is that recent research makes the principles of decision-making accessible, so that anyone who really understands them can make better, more confident decisions.

The Origins of This Book

We began our decision coaching when we were both professors and researchers at the University of Chicago's Center for Decision Research in the late 1970s. The center had been founded in 1977 by the late Professor Hillel Einhorn in the belief that new work in decision psychology had much to offer to professional decision-makers. It has made the University of Chicago the acknowledged leader among business schools in this new field.

Our first major project outside the university began in the fall of 1980 when a group representing Illinois state judges called the school. We were able to help the judges, and since then we have addressed not only business people but also physicians, lawyers, hospital administrators, government officials, and educators. Even high school principals of the Archdiocese of Chicago have found our ideas useful. MBA candidates, investing in an expensive degree, increasingly choose to take courses in the new decision-making. A growing number of business schools are establishing such courses, and Cornell has become the second university in America to have founded a center for behavioral research in decision-making.

Most Decision-Makers Commit the Same Kinds of Errors

The decision research of the last two decades has shown that people in numerous fields tend to make the same kinds of decision-making mistakes. So whatever kind of decision you have to make, you can probably use the insights a small group of researchers have developed to prevent those mistakes.

We have highlighted the most common errors in the following ten "decision traps." We will look at each in turn in the chapters that follow. You'll find that these errors (and other, related mistakes that we'll introduce) plague different parts of your decision-making process. Our goal in this book is to show you how to shape your decision approach so as to avoid each of them. If you do that, we'll guarantee a good decision-making process. And guaranteeing a good decision-making process is as close as anyone can come to assuring good decision outcomes.

Here is our summary of the ten most dangerous decision traps:

1. **Plunging In**—Beginning to gather information and reach conclusions without first taking a few minutes to think about the crux of the issue you're facing or to think through how you believe decisions like this one should be made.

2. **Frame Blindness**—Setting out to solve the wrong problem because you have created a mental framework for

your decision, with little thought, that causes you to over-look the best options or lose sight of important objectives.

3. **Lack of Frame Control**—Failing to consciously define the problem in more ways than one or being unduly influenced by the frames of others.

4. **Overconfidence in Your Judgment**—Failing to collect key factual information because you are too sure of your assumptions and opinions.

5. **Shortsighted Shortcuts**—Relying inappropriately on "rules of thumb" such as implicitly trusting the most readily available information or anchoring too much on convenient facts.

6. **Shooting From the Hip**—Believing you can keep straight in your head all the information you've discovered, and therefore "winging it" rather than following a systematic procedure when making the final choice.

7. **Group Failure**—Assuming that with many smart people involved, good choices will follow automatically, and therefore failing to manage the group decision-making process.

8. **Fooling Yourself About Feedback**—Failing to interpret the evidence from past outcomes for what it really says, either because you are protecting your ego or because you are tricked by hindsight.

9. **Not Keeping Track**—Assuming that experience will make its lessons available automatically, and therefore failing to keep systematic records to track the results of your decisions and failing to analyze these results in ways that reveal their key lessons.

10. **Failure to Audit Your Decision Process**—Failing to create an organized approach to understanding your own

decision-making, so you remain constantly exposed to all the above mistakes.

In simple decisions—say, whether to return a phone call—you probably do not need to worry about these decision traps. Some people spend too much time on the phone with time-wasters, and need to learn a few rules of thumb that will help them keep free. They don't need to study our decision traps to do that.

But in big decisions—the decisions that determine the success of your life and that of those around you—the decision traps frequently cause havoc. In the course of a job search, for instance, all ten decision traps could contribute to misery. Many people suffer from FRAME BLINDNESS about what they're looking for; most suffer from OVERCONFIDENCE ABOUT JUDGMENTS regarding the kinds of jobs that are available; many PLUNGE IN and take the first job offered without evaluating how a decision to take a new job should be made.

People make these mistakes partly because their emotions run high when they seek a job. But great athletes also cope with highly emotional situations. Your job search is no more stressful than what faces the football player who must kick a game-deciding field goal. Well-coached, disciplined athletes prevail because they learn a systematic approach to their sport; it becomes part of them, and they become good enough so that they can trust themselves under pressure.

This book, therefore, will not only list the traps to avoid but also teach you the *process* of decision-making as a coach teaches the process of swimming. With practice you'll not only learn the rules for making great decisions, but also make the process part of you. When you've got a good process and you have internalized it, you can rise above stress and confusion.

A well-trained decision-maker will sometimes make a

mistake, just as a great athlete can lose a big game. But if you teach yourself an excellent decision-making process and practice it, you can succeed with consistency. This book, we believe, can help ensure decisions that regularly enable you to triumph.

DECISION
TRAPS

Chapter I
An Excellent Decision-Making Process

Nothing is more difficult, and therefore more precious, than to be able to decide.

NAPOLEON,
Maxims, 1804

Athletes set new records every year for at least one important reason: Coaches have learned that excellent athletic performance depends on processes they can analyze systematically. Year by year, in almost every sport, the best coaches learn more about the processes involved in great athletic achievement as well as better ways to teach these processes.

Becoming a good decision-maker is like becoming a good athlete. You need to examine the process of decision-making systematically. You need to know how each part of the process contributes to an excellent decision, and know the errors associated with each part. And you need to work consistently on eliminating the errors you still commit in each phase. For example, managers whom we've trained are alert to overconfidence in their judgments. They avoid rationalizing mistakes in past decisions. If they have come to liken their business to a football game, they constantly check to see whether that metaphor still fits their business's real problems.

The right way to play golf often violates your intuition. (Most beginners for example think they should bend their arms as they swing a golf club.) So also, the right way to make decisions often violates your natural inclinations. Good decision-makers have learned that what they "know," even about a field where they are recognized experts, is often wrong. As Ron van Beaumont, head of senior management training at Royal Dutch/Shell put it, "Our executives have to learn when to *distrust* their judgments."

In this chapter we describe the key elements of an excellent decision-making process and introduce the metadecision, an important first step that should take place before you've even completely defined the question to be decided. Then in the rest of the book we look closely at each of the major parts of the process in turn, to explain the decision traps you are likely to confront and how to overcome them.

The Key Elements

The decision-making process can be broken down into four main elements. Every good decision-maker must, consciously or unconsciously, go through each of them.

They are:

1. **Framing:** Structuring the question. This means defining what must be decided and determining in a preliminary way what criteria would cause you to prefer one option over another. In framing, good decision-makers think about the viewpoint from which they and others will look at the issue and decide which aspects they consider important and which they do not. Thus they inevitably simplify the world.

For example, in deciding whom to promote you may simply define the problem as: "Selecting the person whose leadership is likely to produce the best performance in the work group." Note that this viewpoint pushes other aspects of the issue into the background, such as ability to connect with other parts of the organization, rapport with external clients, or rewarding the employee who has worked hardest or who has most seniority.

2

2. **Gathering Intelligence:** Seeking both the knowable facts and the reasonable estimates of "unknowables" that you will need to make the decision. Good decision-makers manage intelligence-gathering with deliberate effort to avoid such failings as overconfidence in what they currently believe and the tendency to seek information that confirms their biases. As Will Rogers said, "It's not what we don't know that causes trouble. It's what we know that ain't so."

3. **Coming to Conclusions:** Sound framing and good intelligence don't guarantee a wise decision. People cannot consistently make good decisions using seat-of-the-pants judgment alone, even with excellent data in front of them. A systematic approach forces you to examine many aspects and often leads to better decisions than hours of unorganized thinking would.

For example, numerous studies have shown that novices as well as professionals make more accurate judgments when they follow systematic rules than when they rely on their intuitive judgment alone.

4. **Learning (or Failing to Learn) from Feedback:** Everyone needs to establish a system for learning from the results of past decisions. This usually means keeping track of what you expected would happen, systematically guarding against self-serving explanations, then making sure you review the lessons your feedback has produced the next time a similar decision comes along.

At minimum, managers should sit down for a few hours twice a year with their associates to look back. Have they been collecting enough data to keep track of the lessons of experience? What have they learned in the past six months? How should it change their future work?

3

These four phases provide the backbone of almost any decision process. Unlike the parts of a golf swing or other athletic effort, however, the phases of the decision process need not be carried out one after the other. Indeed, information discovered in the "intelligence-gathering" phase should often inspire you to go back and reframe your decision. Moreover, a complex problem (the relocation of your business, for instance) may demand a series of smaller decisions, each of which will involve several framing decisions, several intelligence-gathering efforts, and several coming-to-conclusions steps.

But you should think about each of these aspects of your decision separately. You can't guard against the characteristic errors of each part unless you learn to recognize which part of the decision you are working on at a given moment. Often avoiding these errors is easy once you have learned to recognize the stages and traps. A good golf swing or swimming stroke is no harder to execute than a poor one. The same holds true for a good decision process.

Decision Trap Number 1:

Plunging In—Beginning to gather information and reach conclusions without first taking a few minutes to think about the crux of the issue you're facing or to think through how you believe decisions like this one should be made.

Where Do You Spend Your Time?

Looking at the decision-making process this way may forever change your work habits. After introducing the four elements of decision-making in our seminars, we usually ask managers where they spend their time. The bulk of their time is typically devoted to intelligence gathering and coming to conclusions, and the least time is spent on framing. Almost all experience anxiety, frustration, and conflict with others before a decision is reached. To make matters worse, little time is usually devoted to postmortems and other ways of learning from experience.

At the end of our seminars, these same people tell us they are going to focus more on framing and on learning from experience. They are going to delegate information-gathering, because they will have a frame with which to tell people what to gather and how. With a good frame, they will also be able to spend less time on the choice itself. Subsequent discussions have shown that this is what actually happens, at least to the managers who we keep in touch with. They experience less aggravation and conflict, and find group meetings more productive and even enjoyable.

The Metadecision

The four major parts of the decision process consume almost all of a good decision-maker's time. At the very beginning, however, you should make choices about the decision process itself—choices that are likely to determine the character of the whole effort. We call these choices the "metadecision." ("Meta" is a Greek prefix denoting here "beyond" or "transcending.")

A wise and timely metadecision can help you avoid Decision Trap Number 1: Plunging In. When you start work on any major issue, you should spend a few minutes (and occasionally a few hours) thinking about the larger issues you are facing. A metadecision involves asking questions like "What is the crux of this issue? In general, how do I believe decisions like this one *should* be made? How much time should I spend on each phase—as a first guess."

If you're considering buying a house for the first time, for instance, you might reflect that the most important part of the decision process will be a series of separate intelligence-gathering efforts—learning about financing options, evaluating various neighborhoods, and finally looking at specific houses. Finding an excellent new home will depend on managing all this intelligence-gathering well.

Often the excellence or sloppiness in decision-making is established in the metadecision that takes place, usually without the decision-maker even knowing it, before framing really begins. The metadecision should be distinct from the actual framing of the decision. You should think about the general *nature* of the decision to buy (or not buy) a new house even before you try to frame precisely what kind of house you want and how much you want to spend.

So before any major decision process is launched, review the Metadecision Questions in the accompanying box. The first two questions are the most crucial. The others serve to illuminate them.

Most decision-makers fail to focus on making the right metadecision. They fall into Decision Trap Number 1: They PLUNGE IN to the decision process. Negotiators, for example, may fail to ask themselves *how* they should decide the right response to their adversary's proposal. Money-losing companies may not ask themselves *what is the crux* of the issue of reviving the business. Companies discussing new products

6

METADECISION QUESTIONS

What's the crux or primary difficulty in this issue? In which of the key elements of the decision process (page 2) does it lie?

In general, how should decisions like this one be made? (e.g. alone or in groups; intuitively or analytically, etc.)

Does this decision greatly affect other decisions?

Must this decision be made at all? Does it need to be made now? Should it be made by me? What parts can I delegate or do jointly?

How much time have decisions like this one taken in the past? How long should this decision take? When should it be made? Are the deadlines arbitrary or real?

Can I proceed sequentially from framing to intelligence-gathering to coming to conclusions, or must I move back and forth among the parts of the decision process on this issue?

Where should I concentrate my time and resources? How much time should I expect to spend on each phase of the decision process? Do I face a difficult job framing this choice? Will intelligence-gathering be the biggest challenge? Will I have difficulty making the decision rationally even after I've completed the framing and intelligence-gathering?

Can I draw on feedback from related decisions and experiences I've faced in the past to make this decision better?

What are my own skills, biases, and limitations in dealing with an issue like this? Do I need to bring in other points of view? Which other points of view would be helpful?

How would a more experienced decision-maker whom I admire handle this issue?

may not think through how new product development decisions *should* be managed. Nothing else can yield more improvement in less time than making more thoughtful metadecisions. At the end of the metadecision you should have a good sense of which phases are most important, and how much time and resources each deserves.

How a Metadecision Transformed Pepsi-Cola

Since few executives have been trained in decision-making, few think deliberately about the decision process and how to handle each step. But many executives have discovered for themselves some excellent decision-making techniques, and some know how to make an excellent metadecision—especially when they can sense their organizations are suffering from the ill-effects of HAVING PLUNGED IN.

John Sculley, now the chairman of Apple Computer, demonstrated the power of a good metadecision when he served as vice president of marketing for Pepsi-Cola in the 1970s when Pepsi was running a distant second to Coca-Cola. In Pepsi's case, Sculley's good metadecision transformed the organization's competitive position.

Sculley recalls in his autobiography, *Odyssey*, that Pepsi-Cola executives believed for many years—rightly—that Coca-Cola's distinctive, hourglass-shaped bottle was "Coke's most important competitive advantage."

"The bottle design nearly became the product itself," Sculley recalls. "It made Coke easier to stack, more comfortable to grip, and more sturdy to withstand a vending machine's drop. As much a part of this country as Mom and apple pie, it was the only company logo a person could pick up in his hand."

Pepsi-Cola executives had plunged into a series of efforts to compete with Coke's bottle. They approached packaging, Sculley says, "within the competitor's framework." They "spent millions of dollars and many years" studying new bottle designs. But although the Pepsi-Cola "swirl" bottle, introduced in 1958, served as the company's standard packaging for nearly two decades, it could never achieve the recognition of the Coke bottle. Pepsi wasn't learning from its own or from Coca-Cola's experience. It was weakly imitating Coke.

Then Sculley realized that the issue was being handled incorrectly. He didn't immediately prescribe a new direction, or even order his staff to think about redefining the problem. Instead, he made a metadecision. In other words, he asked and answered the crucial question, "How should problems like this be approached?"

Perhaps Sculley didn't ask all the metadecision questions listed in the metadecision box on page 7. But it's clear that he asked several of them in one way or another, and you can easily see how the entire list would have helped point Pepsi's decision-making process in the right direction:

What's the crux of the issue?
> Coke's bottle. We need to "nullify that particular strength." (*Odyssey*, page 20)

How should decisions like this one be made?
> By seeking to "shift the ground rules" to alter the whole playing field if possible, by "pulling back and asking what the customer really wanted." (*Odyssey*, page 21)

How much time should this decision take?
> This decision is central to Pepsi's entire market position. We can take years if necessary to make it correctly.

9

Can I draw on feedback from related decisions and expe-
~~riences I've faced in the past to make this decision better?~~
The feedback only shows that we're not handling this
issue right.

Sculley realized that the company simply didn't know
enough about consumers to determine what they really
wanted, and therefore it couldn't conduct its marketing decision process in the right way. So before he even tried to assign
the bottle question to a new task force, he created an opportunity to learn from a kind of feedback the company had never
used before: He launched a careful test to study how families
actually consumed Pepsi and other soft drinks *in their homes*.

The company allowed 350 families to order soft drinks
weekly in whatever quantity they wanted at discount prices.
"To our astonishment," Sculley recalls, "we discovered that
no matter how much Pepsi they ordered, they would always
consume it." Sculley had discovered what all marketers now
recognize as a key fact about snack foods—however much you
can persuade people to buy, that's how much they'll eat.

"It dawned on me," he says, "that what we needed to do
was design packages that made it easier for people to get more
soft drinks into the home."

Now Sculley could properly frame the issue of competing
with the Coca-Cola bottle: "It became obvious," he continues,
"that we should change the rules of the competition entirely.
We should launch new, larger, and more varied packages."

Pepsi began a new intelligence-gathering phase, decided to
launch a new group of larger packages, and established new
systems to learn from feedback in the stores to refine the
packaging strategy still further.

10

The Fruits of Stepping Back

The results were dramatic. Coca-Cola couldn't convert its famed hourglass silhouette bottle into a larger container. Pepsi's market share expanded dramatically. Indeed, Pepsi drove the long-unassailable "Coke bottle" into extinction in the U.S. market. Today Pepsi-Cola is fiercely competitive in U.S. supermarkets with Coke.

And it happened largely because Sculley avoided a decision trap into which all other Pepsi executives had fallen: He didn't PLUNGE IN to the decision of developing a competitor to the Coke bottle, but took time to contemplate how strategic decisions like that should ideally be made.

Good metadecision thinking at the start of a decision-making process led John Sculley to a brilliant solution. It can do the same for you.

Part I

DECISION-
FRAMING

Chapter 2
The Power of Frames

Seek simplicity, then distrust it.
ALFRED NORTH WHITEHEAD

Everyone must simplify the world. When you begin even the most mundane decision process—for example, choosing a new television set—you can never consider *all* the information that might be relevant. (What features will you want over the next ten years? Are you getting the best price? Will it give you eyestrain?)

Everyone, from the greatest genius to the most ordinary clerk, has to adopt mental frameworks that simplify and structure the information encountered in the world. If you shop wisely for a television, for instance, you'll probably start by listing a few key characteristics you want, then decide to select a set by visiting a few stores, talking to a few friends, or reading *Consumer Reports* magazine. However you approach the decision, some aspects will inevitably escape your analysis.

We call the mental structures people create to simplify and organize the world decision "frames." Frames keep complexity within the dimensions our minds can manage. No one can make a rational decision without framing. Television buyers who fail to construct a framework for their purchases, for example, will find themselves easily manipulated by the salespeople in stores.

But beware: Any frame leaves us with only a partial view of the problem. Often people simplify in ways that actually force them to choose the wrong alternatives.

15

Decision Trap Number 2:

Frame Blindness—Setting out to solve the wrong problem because you have created a mental framework for your decision, with little thought, that causes you to overlook the best options or lose sight of important objectives.

Frame Blindness Destroys U.S. Automakers' Genius

Consider how U.S. automakers framed the problem of improving manufacturing efficiency from the 1940s through the 1970s. The industry had taken pride in its manufacturing ever since the introduction of the assembly line. After World War II it began to use the newly emerging "operations research" tools to find "optimal" solutions to manufacturing problems. One such problem was: How many of a single car model (for example, a four-door sedan) should we make in one production run before we change over to another model (a station wagon, perhaps)?

Setting up heavy equipment such as stamping dies to make a different model required considerable time—several hours at least. Thus, the industry wanted to minimize the number of changeovers, even if that meant keeping large inventories of each model to satisfy dealer demand between production runs. The sophisticated calculations called for production runs as long as 1,000 or more cars of a single model.

16

The automakers based production runs on these seemingly sophisticated calculations for decades. They made every manufacturing improvement within a frame that assumed changeover time was fixed at something like six to eight hours. U.S. engineers had set boundaries that implicitly assumed—for no clear reason except that they needed to simplify the world to analyze it—that one could not much reduce model changeover time. In other words, their frame bounded out the idea that changeover time itself could be cut.

The Japanese auto industry framed the question of manufacturing efficiency quite differently. Japanese automakers, especially Toyota, realized that they could make their *entire system* more efficient by reducing changeover time. They could utilize their assembly lines more fully, carry smaller inventories, offer a larger variety of models, and respond faster to customer orders.

So the Japanese set out to speed up changeovers. In the early 1950s, their times had differed little from U.S. automakers'. Two decades later, while U.S. companies still used analyses that assumed changeovers took nearly an entire shift, changeovers in Japan required only a few minutes. By the mid-1980s, one Toyota plant could change models in as little as forty-four seconds.

U.S. manufacturers eventually woke up, and today they measure model changeover time in minutes and seconds, too. But even today Toyota saves hundreds of dollars per car over its U.S. rivals, in part because Toyota production lines change models yet more quickly and efficiently than U.S. lines.

The U.S. automakers were caught in Decision Trap Number 2, FRAME BLINDNESS. They unknowingly set out to solve the wrong problem. They had defined their problem with insufficient thought about implicit assumptions, causing them to overlook the best options.

Understanding Frames

FRAME BLINDNESS is common. No frame—indeed no way of thinking—can consider all possibilities. Thus no one can completely avoid the dangers of framing. But many professionals pay dearly because they don't even know the problem exists.

The analogy of a window frame nicely illustrates the difficulties. Architects choose where to put windows to give a desired view. But no single window can reveal the entire panorama.

When you choose which window to look through—or even if you decide to keep track of what's happening through three different windows—you can never be sure in advance that you'll get the most useful picture.

The framing of a decision inevitably sets boundaries; it controls what is in and what is out. Moreover, not all elements that are "in" will be treated equally. Our frames tend to focus us on certain things while leaving others obscured.

For example, suppose an advertising agency simply asks, "How can we cut costs?" or "How do other ad agencies cut costs?" Those questions will point employees toward simple cost-cutting techniques such as delaying office equipment purchases and perhaps laying off unproductive staff. Now suppose the same agency adds this additional question to its frame: "How do other kinds of businesses cut costs without reducing quality?" This opens a window on possibilities for more creative changes such as limiting the "menu" of services offered, recycling discarded ideas from one campaign into others, etc.

18

The Strength of Frames

Frames have enormous power. <u>The way people frame a problem greatly influences the solution they will ultimately choose</u>. And the frames that people or organizations routinely use for their problems control how they will react to almost everything they encounter.

Framing traps indeed can turn managers of outstanding potential into terrible blunderers. One large consumer products company promoted its talented marketing vice president to chief executive, for example. But he remained trapped in what we call "the marketing frame"—the view that he always had to concentrate on understanding and meeting customers' wants. As president, he decreed the company would bring out dozens of new items, new models, and new colors; he ensured that every outlet would carry so much inventory that nothing ، would ever run out.

Not surprisingly, the company could not stand the strain of this single dominant frame. After a few months, factory managers couldn't meet the CEO's demands without losing control of costs and delivery schedules. Interest charges ballooned because of the vast inventories. After several years of losses, the board of directors had to fire the boss.

As we'll see throughout this book, companies frequently suffer years of losses because they box themselves into sensible-sounding, but fundamentally inappropriate, frames. <u>The best frames will highlight what is important and relegate to the shadows what is not</u>. Though they also simplify reality, winning frames are far more open to unanticipated information than the automakers' operations research frame or the frame of the marketing-vice-president-turned-CEO. We will discuss how to frame decisions properly—and how to utilize more than one frame—in this and the following chapter.

19

Good framing is as much an art as a science, but it is an art that can be learned. The first step is to understand a few of the basic characteristics of frames.

A Frame for Each Problem

When they face a new issue, good decision-makers (and most others as well) create a decision frame specifically designed for dealing with that problem.

Few people are fully aware of the decision frames they're adopting. But you can understand your own decision frames, and if you do you're likely to make better decisions and to recognize more readily when those decisions need to be changed. A top manager's most demanding job is to create, select, and manage the process by which the company selects **winning frames**—ways of looking at problems that focus on the most important aspects of the questions and allow other aspects appropriate attention. Winning frames lead to wise choices.

To understand your own decision frame, start by thinking about:

1. the boundaries you've set on the problem,

2. the reference points you're using to define success and failure, and

3. the yardsticks you're using to measure with.

Then, to get a fuller picture, think about the metaphors or deeper frames that underlie your thinking, either consciously or unconsciously. (For instance, some shoppers buying automobiles approach the decision as a wrestling match with the dealer for the lowest possible price; others think more in terms of a lasting partnership with the dealer.) Think about the ideas

20

you've brought to the decision from your culture, occupation, education, and family background. Often you'll want to look at your decision through alternative frames before you make a final choice.

This sounds like a big job, and it is a big job the first time you do it. This chapter will deal with each of these issues in turn. Then the next chapter will offer detailed methods for analyzing your own and others' frames. In the long run, skilled decision-making takes no more effort than unskilled decision-making.

Boundaries

Boundaries are among a problem frame's simplest elements. Yet you probably don't understand the boundaries you draw in framing even small decisions. Try this exercise developed by Daniel Kahneman of the University of California at Berkeley and Amos Tversky of Stanford University to demonstrate how boundaries affect decisions.

Start by putting yourself in the following situation:

Situation A: You have decided to see a play and bought a ticket for thirty dollars. As you enter the theater, you discover that you have lost the ticket. The seat was not marked and the ticket cannot be recovered. Would you pay thirty dollars for another ticket to see the play (assuming you still have enough cash)?

We have not told you anything about the play (except that for some reason you were originally willing to pay thirty dollars to see it). But try anyway to decide whether you would pay thirty dollars for another ticket.

Once you've made a decision, consider a second situation:

Situation B: You have decided to see a play where admission is thirty dollars per ticket, but you have not yet purchased the ticket. As you enter the theater you discover that you have lost thirty dollars from your wallet. Would you still pay thirty dollars for a ticket to see the play (assuming you have enough cash left)?

How would you choose? Would you buy a ticket for thirty dollars?

We have posed Situation A (the lost ticket) and Situation B (the lost cash) to over 100 managers, each of whom saw only one version. The results:

When managers are told the ticket is lost, 38 percent said they would be unwilling to pay thirty dollars for another ticket to see the play.

When managers are told the cash is lost, only 17 percent said they would be unwilling to pay the thirty dollars.

Yet it shouldn't matter! After all, in both cases you've suffered an equal loss and you are equally poor. So why shouldn't you be equally willing—or unwilling—to buy another ticket? People decide differently because they frame the decision differently when it's a lost ticket instead of lost cash.

Many people who are told the ticket is lost feel that buying another would be equivalent to spending sixty dollars to see the play.

In contrast, the cash lost in Situation B has little connection to the play in people's minds. They instinctively draw a boundary around the question, "Should I spend money to buy a ticket?" And the lost cash is outside that boundary while the lost ticket is inside it.

In business, the boundaries of people's daily tasks can powerfully frame people's view of their entire company or of business generally. One automotive products company, for instance, was losing money in the early 1980s. A parent-company task force asked key managers to investigate the decline. They found:

—The marketing group thought the problem was due to lack of advertising and promotional support.

—The sales group blamed lack of promotion and dealer-support programs.

—The manufacturing and distribution group blamed inaccurate forecasting by the marketing and sales groups, which caused poor production planning and high costs.

—The finance department blamed budget overruns by all departments, and unreliable forecasts from the marketing group.

—The legal department blamed a lack of new franchising and licensing agreements, which meant the company lacked new products.

Managers in most fields tend to draw narrow boundaries around the questions they think about, and their solution to any business problem is likely to come from within those boundaries. The example is reminiscent of the Indian fable of the six blind men and the elephant: each felt only a part.

What was really going on? The task force concluded that the subsidiary's president had discouraged interdepartmental cooperation. He had constantly criticized each department and had encouraged departments to criticize each other. Top managers must overcome the narrow frames of different departments and make them feel like part of a whole. The president of this company had failed to do that, and thus had failed in his job as a whole. The parent company fired him. A new president refused to get involved in departmental squabbles, and the company soon reported profits again.

Sometimes a takeover raid—or the threat of one—produces great value because it breaks boundaries in managers' decision frames. Managers may have "bounded out" of consideration

23

the closing of money-losing plants, selling underutilized real estate, or laying off unproductive workers. But when corporate raiders knock on the door, or a disaster strikes, many such boundaries evaporate.

On the other hand, sometimes the problem is a *failure* to draw a boundary that should be drawn. For example, many managers commit the "sunk-cost fallacy": They permit past investments to influence today's decisions when they should bound such costs out of consideration. Careful analysis at a major U.S. steel company showed it could save hundreds of thousands of dollars every year by replacing its hot-metal mixing technology, which required that metal be heated twice, with direct-pouring technology, in which the metal was only heated once. But the move was approved only after considerable delay because senior engineers complained that the analysis "did not include the cost of the hot-metal mixers"— which had been purchased for $3 million just a few years previously.

A rationally drawn boundary would have excluded the cost of past investments from consideration. The company had already spent that money, and the bonds on its balance sheet to pay for the hot-metal mixers would remain there whether the new direct-pouring technology was adopted or not. Rational decisions should be based on comparisons between *future* gains and *future* costs (including the salvage value of the hot-metal mixers, but *not* their original price). However, people are reluctant to let themselves feel that they made a mistake, and mixing up boundaries makes it easy for them to avoid it.

The "marketing frame" is an example of a winning frame created by extending boundaries. It achieved well-deserved popularity in the United States after World War II.

Prior to that time, corporations had felt it was their job to design good products and motivate the sales force to sell them.

24

But in the late 1940s, production capacity exceeded demand in many U.S. industries. Even well-designed products might be difficult to sell. Businesses had to talk to consumers to draw out what the consumers really wanted—and learning directly from customers had traditionally been outside of their frames.

Under the marketing frame, consumers' opinion became central to virtually every stage of the new product development process. Companies did market research to determine what customers wanted. They studied their ways of life to figure out where new products could fit in. The new frame risked undervaluing the role of production or research, but on the whole businesses benefited enormously. Hundreds of companies reached new heights of prosperity by adopting the marketing frame.

Reference Points

The reference points—the elements that the decision-maker uses to determine success or failure—can determine decisions almost as much as the frame's boundaries. In a decision frame, the reference point acts like the focal point in a painting or the origin of a graph. Just as skilled painters choose the best focal point on their canvas, so should skilled professionals choose the best reference point in managing their problems.

One manager in Texas discovered the importance of controlling reference points in 1983, when he faced deep dissatisfaction over salary increases that averaged only 5 percent. His company's profits had recently increased nearly 20 percent, and the employees were using both the company's profit increase and the inflationary increases of the 1970s as reference points. The manager was able to change his employees' reference points through a little research. He learned that the company's major competitor in the same area had offered only 3 percent salary increases and in addition, rumors of layoffs at the competitor were in the air. He emphasized this to his employees, along with his own company's lifetime job security policy. Dissatisfaction quieted quickly.

Many people don't think about their reference points. They fail to realize how reference points can affect their decisions. But sometimes the choice of reference point can have life-or-death consequences. For example, a study published in the *New England Journal of Medicine* showed that doctors chose different treatments for a hypothetical case of lung cancer depending on whether the outcome was posed in terms of the likelihood of living or the likelihood of dying. Researchers asked 167 doctors to imagine they had lung cancer. Half were told:

> Of 100 people having surgery, 10 will die during surgery, 32 will have died by one year, and 66 will have died by five years. Of 100 people having radiation therapy, none will die during treatment, 23 will die by one year, and 78 will die by five years. Which treatment would you prefer?

The other half were told:

> Of 100 people having surgery, 90 will survive the surgery, 68 will survive past one year, and 34 will survive through five years. Of 100 people having radiation therapy, all will survive the treatment, 77 will survive one year, and 22 will survive past five years. Which treatment would you prefer?

Of the first group (those told "10 will die . . ." etc.), about half chose radiation therapy and half chose surgery. Of the second group (those told "90 will survive . . ."), however, fully 84 percent chose surgery. Even physicians—who might be expected to know how to think dispassionately about such subjects—can't make medical decisions without being influenced by the reference point in the problem frame. When the reference point is survival (and attention is drawn to the

26

chance to continue living), the risk of surgery is viewed much more favorably.

Probably the best way for doctors to deal with this problem in presenting choices to patients is to offer the facts with *both* reference points. For instance, doctors could say:

> "Of 100 people having surgery, 10 will die during treatment and 90 will survive, 32 will have died by the end of one year and 68 will survive . . ." etc.

Use of the wrong reference point can turn good organizations into mediocre ones. For example, many major British companies fell into low productivity, shoddy design, and general lack of innovation in the 1950s and '60s when they continued to use each other's performances as their reference points instead of comparing themselves with the excellent innovations developing overseas. On the other hand, a shift of reference point can reinvigorate a business, as U.S. automakers found when they shifted from constantly comparing product quality among themselves to comparing their performance to the best global rivals.

Shifting reference points can also work to sell and frame a price increase. Storer Cable Communications sent the following notice to subscribers in Louisville, Kentucky:

> It's not often you get good news instead of a bill, but we've got some for you. If you've heard all those rumors about your basic cable rate going up $10 or more a month, you can relax: *it's not going to happen!* The great news is . . . the rate for basic cable is increasing only $2 a month.

Yardsticks

The yardsticks we use in our decision frames can also cause trouble. Consider this exercise, adapted from Richard Thaler of Cornell University:

27

Situation A: You are in a store about to buy a new watch which will cost $70. As you wait for the sales clerk, a friend comes by and tells you that an identical watch is available in another store two blocks away for $40. You know that the service and reliability of the other store are just as good as this one. Will you travel two blocks to save $30?

Decide yes or no. Then consider a similar situation.

Situation B: You are in a store about to buy a new video camera that costs $800. As you wait for the sales clerk, a friend comes by and tells you that an identical camera is available in another store two blocks away for $770. You know that the service and reliability of the other store are just as good as this one. Will you travel two blocks to save $30?

We have posed a similar question to several hundred managers. In Situation A, about 90 percent say they would travel the two blocks. In Situation B, only 50 percent would travel.

Yet there is no real difference between the two situations. Both boil down to the question of whether you are willing to walk two blocks to save thirty dollars. People, especially savvy managers, should see through the surface of the problem, and *decide the same way in both situations.*

People decide differently because they are accustomed to thinking about savings in percentages, not absolute dollars. But in camera and watch shopping, the percentage yardstick doesn't make sense. You know the two stores are equally reliable. All that counts is what you put in (or take out of) your pocket, which is dollars—not percentages.

It's especially important to control the yardstick when you evaluate employees. Subordinates regularly manipulate yardsticks to frame the thinking of their superiors. For example, if

28

a project budgeted at $100,000 is completed for only $90,000, the employee will express his or her accomplishment as an impressive absolute: "I saved the company $10,000."

If, however, that same $100,000 project costs $110,000, then the same person will minimize the overrun by claiming: "I stayed within 10 percent of the budget."

One Japan Airlines pilot took this tendency to a ridiculous extreme on a flight from Tokyo to San Francisco in 1968. Due to communication failure with the control tower he brought his DC-8 down through low clouds, three miles short of the runway and made a "perfect" water landing—in San Francisco Bay. Luckily, no one was injured. He is reported to have framed his error as a percentage in discussing it with the media: "Considering that I traveled all the way from Tokyo, how much did I miss by?" His superiors weren't entirely persuaded. He was demoted to copilot and restricted to intra-Asian routes.

Metaphors

Boundaries, reference points, and yardsticks are the simpler characteristics of problem frames. You can probably recognize many of the boundaries and most of the reference points and yardsticks in the problem frames you and others create. But boundaries, reference points, yardsticks, and your explicit statements of the problem are only part of the framework that you create in your head to address an issue. Other aspects of the frame are more difficult to perceive.

Metaphors can play a profound role in many people's problem frames. Good decision-makers choose metaphors carefully to highlight important facets of the situation at hand. Poor decision-makers (or decision-makers who are competent only in narrow fields) may automatically use one or two

29

metaphors to frame almost everything. For example, they may frame everything as a football game, a war or a family.

Whenever we use a metaphor intelligently, we think about the current situation or phenomenon (which we understand imperfectly) in terms of another we understand better. Shifting metaphors can especially help us to understand and sometimes alter parts of our frames that come from our upbringing, education, or professional experience.

Here's a powerful example of how a metaphor can create a problem frame: In 1984 James River Corporation, a U.S. manufacturer of such paper products as Northern napkins and bathroom tissue and Brawny paper towels, sought to break into the rich Northeastern market in the United States, where it would face deeply entrenched competition from companies such as Procter & Gamble and Scott Paper. Ronald L. Singer, the vice president-group executive in charge, told an interviewer from the American Marketing Association that he believed marketing was like war:

> "The classical principles of warfare and being combat ready are keys to the success of major marketing campaigns. . . . You need good intelligence, sound planning, security and surprise, concentration of forces, exploitation of breakthroughs, protection of your flanks, and motivation of the troops. That is the way to win wars and beat competitors."

George Patton could hardly have stated the military frame more forcefully. However, words are cheap. Did Singer indeed take military-style actions that were unconventional for new product introduction but natural to his military frame? Yes. Here are some of the steps James River Corporation took to achieve security and surprise:

—The new production facility in Maine was closed to all outsiders.

—Employees were instructed not to discuss the product launch even with family members.

—The project task force was segregated from the rest of the company.

—Absolutely no test marketing was conducted.

These are unusual, even extreme, measures. (They would have been unthinkable for Procter & Gamble, for instance.) To develop your own skills in understanding frames, ask yourself the following questions:

1. What aspects of the business challenge are being highlighted by the military frame?

2. What aspects are being concealed?

3. What are alternative ways to frame the problem of introducing James River's brands in the Northeast?

4. Which of the possible frames best fits the problem?

Here are some answers:
The military frame *highlights competition*—the battle that Procter & Gamble and Scott will wage to defend their territory and the demands that the battle will put on James River employees.

The military frame *conceals the customer*, as an intelligent buyer whose needs must be recognized and satisfied. It treats customers as secondary to competitors; they are merely territory to be fought over and conquered.

You can obtain *alternative ways of framing the problem* of introducing James River paper products in the Northeast by changing metaphors. The complex process of introducing a new brand calls for so much coordination among so many people—many of them unfamiliar with branded-products

31

marketing—that some kind of metaphor is probably vital to communicate the frame to all the people involved. But one alternative approach to framing the product introduction would be *the evolution frame* ("survival of the fittest"). Managers could think of James River's brands as a new species being introduced into an environment where only the fittest will survive. The evolution metaphor shifts the focus from the competitor to the product, from outmaneuvering other brand managers to assuring that your own product is superior in its environment.

Which of the possible frames best fits the problem? Ultimately, the military frame worked well for James River. The company seized a profitable market share in the Northeast in a matter of a year or so. "In the beginning our people regularly laughed at my analogies to D-Day" admits Singer. "After a while they stopped laughing at my General Patton uniform."

James River was trying to penetrate an existing market for a low-technology product with easily identified competitors. This is a zero-sum situation; one person's gain is another's loss. The military frame fits well here. However, it would probably not have worked as well in an expanding market, perhaps for a high-technology product, with many smaller competitors instead of two big ones.

The military frame (and other common metaphors such as a football game) can serve a decision-maker well in a wide variety of situations if the decision-maker has a rich understanding of the variations possible within it. For example, *Marketing Warfare* by Al Ries and Jack Trout describes an array of quite different marketing problems in terms of military metaphors. Rolls-Royce, the super-luxury car company, is described as a guerrilla warrior—it grabs a number of small, nearly invisible outposts in enemy territory. Companies such as Digital Equipment and Mercedes-Benz are described as pursuing a "flanking strategy"—seeking to offer something different from the competition. Leaders such as IBM and Gillette pursue a "defensive battle."

But even a rich array of metaphors from a single area of life has limitations. IBM, for instance, probably could not have become great if it thought of its big-business customers as simply territory to conquer.

Thinking Frames

When someone uses the same mental framework to deal with many different problems, it becomes what we call a **thinking frame**—a frame that the individual applies automatically and uses frequently to structure a wide range of thinking. Many metaphors become thinking frames (especially for people like James River's Ronald L. Singer, who spent twelve years in the Pentagon analyzing the battles of World War II before he joined the paper company).

In addition, every culture teaches its young powerful thinking frames that are more than metaphor. (For example, the ideal of majority rule is a thinking frame for Americans, who attempt to apply it in sports clubs, labor unions, and even in evaluating the "good" and "bad" aspects of foreign cultures.) A person's occupation and education similarly produce powerful thinking frames (such as the "free market" ideology of many economics graduates). And of course many people have thinking styles that reflect different personalities.

Many thinking frames become so deeply ingrained in groups or organizations that people cannot change them when the circumstances call for it. **Cultural frames**, the thinking frames adopted by whole cultures, are often examples of this. Here's an instance of the deep impact of cultural frames

33

recorded by the historian Herodotus over twenty-four centuries ago:

> Darius, when he was King, summoned those Greeks who were with him and asked what sum of money would induce them to make a meal of their dead fathers; and they said nothing would induce them to do this. Darius then summoned the Callatian Indians, who do eat their deceased parents, and asked them how much money they would take to burn their dead fathers in a fire (as the Greeks did); and they raised a great uproar, telling him not to speak of such a thing.

While many business frames are less dramatic than the ways in which different cultures deal with their dead, we shouldn't underestimate the effects of thinking frames on businesses. Corporate leaders often apply metaphors to entire companies, for instance, thereby making the metaphors into thinking frames for the whole corporate culture. The Johnson family, proprietors of S. C. Johnson, Inc. (formerly Johnson Wax), sees its firm as a big family. Sam Johnson, the firm's chief executive, once flew all 500 employees of the firm's seventy-year-old British subsidiary to the United States for a week because he became concerned that they felt undervalued being so distant from their American cousins.

When you find people caught in an inappropriate thinking frame, you may be wasting your time if you try to change it. Just make the best decision you can, and then find a way to sell that decision to them within the context of their own frame. (We'll discuss "aligning" your frame to that of someone you want to influence at the end of the next chapter.)

Misframing

We need a repertoire of thinking frames to make sense of the world. Any thinking frame has built-in dangers, and the more frequently it is used, the more likely it is to be used uncritically.

When your mental framework is coherent, is applied repeatedly to different decisions, and controls what you perceive, then you are likely to use it to misframe decisions. Military-frame companies are in danger of using the military frame to deal with government regulators (who have power the company can't beat with military-style tactics). Family-frame companies may react violently and stubbornly against union attempts to organize their plants (which they see as causing division in the family).

Frames can be dangerous because they play tricks on our minds. They often seem more complete (and hence more appropriate) than in fact they are. All frames simplify and thus contain gaps, and they can keep you from seeing what is missing.

This is one reason we easily lock ourselves into a single frame. It appears complete from inside. Understanding the three key dangers of framing helps prevent misframing:

—Without realizing it, we tend to see reality through one frame at a time. (Most people never see the other perspective if they are not told it is there.)

—Once locked into one frame, it may be difficult to switch.

—Most problems should be examined through more than one frame, but this is difficult.

35

No single frame can capture a complex problem fully. In many cases, no single frame can even capture a complex problem adequately. You often need to use multiple frames, and you should choose your frame or frames carefully. To examine problems through more than one frame, we usually have to try one frame after another.

We'll show both how to choose frames well and how to look at the same problem from more than one frame in the next chapter.

Chapter 3
Winning Frames

The test of a first-rate intelligence is the ability to hold two opposite ideas in mind at the same time and still retain the ability to function.

F. SCOTT FITZGERALD

Most people don't choose frames, they stumble into them. They may realize that they should define and structure their problems with care. But they don't know the skill of framing, so they can't control this process.

This chapter will show you how to manage frames. That means:

—Achieving frame awareness,

—selecting decision frames carefully,

—reframing intelligently when you find yourself using an inadequate frame, and

—matching your own frame to the frames of other people you want to influence.

Know Your Own Frames

The key to sound decision-making is: **Know your own frames.** You need to know how you have simplified your problems. Otherwise, you'll never recognize when you need

37

to reframe and you may lack the self-knowledge necessary to do any reframing well.

The first step to achieving frame awareness is learning how you—and the competition—draw boundaries around problems. For example, many managers have learned how to better frame their competition from Harvard Business School strategy expert Michael Porter. Traditionally, businesses tended to think of "competition" as the struggle with firms producing similar products or services. Porter pointed out that this frame often caused companies to underemphasize other competitive pressures on profit such as their own suppliers (who might be charging them too much), customers (who frequently want to pay less and consume too much service), substitute products, potential entrants, government, employees, etc.

Porter urged each company to think through who its real competitors are. The oil industry, for instance, should think of its key competition as governments, since of every dollar's worth of oil sold, about eighty cents goes to governments in some form of tax. By understanding how they frame the issue of "competition," business people set themselves up to make wiser decisions and become ready to change that frame again when necessary. All business people should understand how they frame (that is, how they simplify) at least a few of the core issues of their businesses.

Know the Frames of Others

A key to communicating with other people, moreover, is: KNOW *THEIR* FRAMES. If you understand how others frame problems, you can tailor your communication to them.

A dramatic example of frame conflict occurred during World War II when U.S. Government agents questioning the loyalty of Japanese-Americans would demand: "Who do you want to win this war, America or Japan?"

Many Japanese-Americans recognized instinctively that the framing of this question was not appropriate to their situation. They loved both countries. So they tried to shift the discussion from a military frame to a family frame, responding: "Who do you want to win when you see your mother and father fighting? You just want them to stop." Their frame was different from their interrogators'.

Decision Trap Number 3:

Lack of Frame Control—Failing to consciously define the problem in more ways than one or being unduly influenced by the frames of others.

Open-Minded Framing

When you approach a new issue, try to remain open-minded about the frame. In the early 1970s, long before "Japanese management" was well known, management guru Peter Drucker pointed out that Japanese corporations seemed especially good at making big decisions. "To the Japanese, the important element in decision-making is *defining the question*," he wrote. "The crucial steps are to decide whether there is a need for a decision and what the decision is about. And it is in this step that the Japanese aim at getting a consensus." In other words, on big questions Japanese companies aimed at consensus on how the decision would be framed. This could take a long time, but it assured that the company would be open to all kinds of relevant information. U.S. corporations

39

tended to expect "their task forces and long-range planning groups to come up with recommendations—that is, to commit themselves to one alternative." Unfortunately, by framing and deciding prematurely, they often guaranteed mistakes no matter how well they performed the remaining steps in selecting and implementing an alternative.

Sometimes open-mindedness has given Japanese companies great flexibility. For example, when Honda Motors set out to enter the U.S. market in 1959, company president Soichiro Honda advised the marketing team to emphasize Honda's larger motorbikes, which closely resembled the motorcycles that were then widely sold in the United States. The company's sales staff itself, however, used the tiny Honda Supercub to travel around Los Angeles because it was cheap. Soon Californians began asking where to get Supercubs. The company listened. Within a few years, it had totally reframed its approach to the U.S. market, focusing on lightweight bikes for ordinary consumers. Honda's openness to the consumer produced an entirely new category of product, causing motorcycle registrations in the U.S. to increase ten-fold from 1960 to 1971.

Knowing When to Reframe

For most decisions, you or your organization already have a frame. You already know how you will hire new employees, how you will select investments, or how you will choose your new advertising campaign. No one should continually reframe every aspect of life.

But perhaps the most important skill in decision-making is to recognize when an issue needs to be reframed. If you continually use an inappropriate frame—that is, if you continue to simplify in ways that blind you to what is most

significant about the problem—you will eventually cast yourself and your organization into deep problems.

The airline industry had to reframe most of its business
when it was deregulated: In the 1960s and '70s, airlines had
managed themselves as a regulated oligopoly. They had
earned regulated profits and passed some on to pilots, flight
attendants, suppliers, etc. But when the U.S. deregulated the
industry and a fierce price war broke out, the frame needed to
be changed. Managers like those at American, Northwest, and
Delta Airlines, who were able to change their frames to suit
their new, highly competitive business environment, pros-
pered. Those who were unwilling or unable (certain managers
at TWA, Braniff, and Pan Am) were nearly ruined.

The need for reframing, however, is not always so obvious.
Recognizing the pivotal role of frames can help a manager
understand when change is needed. One real estate development partnership, for example, had a policy of hiring people
who excelled in sports. It had discovered that athletes possessed the drive and determination needed to push real estate
developments to successful completion.

Then the business began to change. Instead of downtown
high-rises and suburban office parks, the market was calling
for renovation of old factories, warehouses, and apartment
buildings. Managers could not understand why their powerful
staff seemed less effective and more frustrated. One partner,
himself a former athlete, realized the truth: The company's
approach to hiring (the way it framed hiring decisions) no
longer fit the business. Although the self-confidence of
athletes could push government agencies and contractors to
action, it wasn't working in relocating tenants and coping with
the surprises found in old buildings. He left the company;
when last we heard, his friends were still struggling with a
now-unfriendly environment.

41

Steps in Reframing

To reframe, you must:

1. understand your current frame and its sources,

2. generate alternative frames, and

3. select the most appropriate.

If you can't find one single frame that is most appropriate, use several of the alternative frames. (We'll discuss how to do this later in the chapter.)

Understanding Your Current Frame

The following Frame Analysis Worksheet will help you understand your current frame. Usually, you don't consciously think about your frame. Thus, you may not find the questions easy to answer. Instead of answering the questions one after the other, you'll probably do better to skip around and enter ideas as they come to you.

To get started, try this suggestion for defining the boundaries of a frame: Start by thinking of alternatives that you automatically exclude but a colleague or competitor would not. You may be completely right to exclude them, but you are drawing boundaries differently from your colleague or competitor. (You may also want to ask what possibilities your view includes that another perspective bounds out.)

The slogan that the last question asks for may be something like Ronald L. Singer's comment: "The classical principles of warfare are keys to the success of major marketing campaigns."

Use a sheet like this to analyze either a frame you are using now, a frame you are considering, or the frame of someone you must communicate with.

FRAME ANALYSIS WORKSHEET

The issue or issues the frame addresses (in a few words):

What boundaries do I (we) (they) put on the question? In other words, what aspects of the situation do I (we) (they) leave out of consideration?

What yardsticks do I (we) (they) use to measure success?

What reference points do I (we) (they) use to measure success?

What metaphors—if any—do I (we) (they) use in thinking about this issue?

Why do I (we) (they) think about this question the way I (we) (they) do?

What does the frame emphasize?

What does it minimize?

Do other people in the _____ industry (fill in your own field) think about this question differently from the way I (we) (they) do?

Can I (we) (they) summarize my (our) (their) frame in a slogan?

You need not complete the whole worksheet before starting to reframe; in fact, the reframing exercises discussed below will often help you fill in the areas on the worksheet where you initially have trouble. Page 45 shows a Frame Analysis Worksheet fully filled in by a fairly rational buyer seeking a new car.

Challenging Your Frame

The key step in reframing a question is to recognize that your frame is not the only one available and that others may be better.

Use the following frame-busting techniques to start generating alternative frames:

1. *Challenge yourself.* Start by challenging the actions you would normally take on this issue. Ask whether each of your own actions makes sense. Suppose the issue is hiring computer programmers and you always start the hiring process by placing an ad in the *New York Times*. Does that really aim your message at the candidates you want to hear from?

If the answer is "No," then ask how the frame you had used for the decision in the past caused you to take the wrong steps. You may have uncovered a **misalignment** of your frame.

2. *Seek other opinions.* Have someone else challenge your frame for you. Seeing your frame is sometimes like seeing your nose—others do it better than you do. Seek a devil's advocate to review your approach to the problem and criticize your reasoning. (Unfortunately, the best devil's advocates are often people we don't really like. We most

Use a sheet like this to analyze either a frame you are using now, a frame you are considering, or the frame of someone you must communicate with.

FRAME ANALYSIS WORKSHEET

The issue or issues the frame addresses (in a few words):

Buying a new car.

What boundaries do I (we) (they) put on the question? In other words, what aspects of the situation do I (we) (they) leave out of consideration?

1. Won't consider a used car or a foreign one.
2. Won't be influenced by financing terms.
3. Won't consider leasing.

What yardsticks do I (we) (they) use to measure success?

1. Frequency of problems once the car is purchased.
2. Total operating cost per mile.

What reference points do I (we) (they) use to measure success?

1. Frequency of problems reported for comparable Japanese cars.
2. Sense of partnership with the dealer that was achieved on a previous vehicle.
3. Usefulness of other people's vehicles on camping vacations.

What metaphors—if any—do I (we) (they) use in thinking about this issue?

None.

Why do I (we) (they) think about this question the way I (we) (they) do?

1. Family has always bought cars seeking to minimize life-cycle cost.
2. Unpredictability of future income suggests cautious spending.

What does the frame emphasize?

Meeting the needs of the family at the right price.

What does it minimize?

Leasing options, used car opportunities, and image or cachet.

Do other people in the consumers _____ industry (fill in your own field) think about this question differently from the way I (we) (they) do?

Yes, some place greater emphasis on minimizing the dealer's markup, others place greater emphasis on options. Many put greater emphasis on monthly payment. Others drive for pleasure or to convey a lifestyle image.

Can I (we) (they) summarize my (our) (their) frame in a slogan?

Get the most car for the least money and aggravation.

Here's a sample of a Frame Analysis Worksheet filled in by a fairly savvy consumer getting ready to buy a car.

enjoy people who share our views and who therefore are least likely to see the frames they share with us.)

3. *Role-play your adversaries.* If a decision involves competitors, take their viewpoint or assign a subgroup of the task force to that role. This is a time-tested technique.

4. *Welcome diversity.* Try to include people with different thinking styles on the team that's considering the issue.

5. *Brainstorming.* Have one member of your group stand at a blackboard. Other members are encouraged to call out suggestions for changing your approach to the problem at hand. The person at the blackboard writes *all* suggestions on the board. No criticism is allowed. Then after the brainstorming session the ideas can be evaluated.

6. *Lateral thinking.* Try to sidestep the problem by looking at it from a different angle. For instance, suppose your people complain about the slow elevators in your building. Rather than think about speeding up the elevators (i.e., trying to solve the problem as posed), you might try to change people's *perceptions* about how long they wait. Adding mirrors next to the elevators, or bulletin boards, or music might solve the problem more cheaply than adding more powerful elevators.

7. *Synectics.* Try to think via analogy. When engineers first tried to build airplanes or strong, tall structures, they derived inspiration from biological analogies such as birds flying (or gliding) and bees building sturdy hives. The essence of synectics is to join seemingly unrelated elements—such as beehives and architectural design. By moving away from the problem to a distantly related phenomenon and then trying to analogize, powerful ideas may result. Try it for yourself: What can a Swiss army knife

teach you about how to organize your division? (Think of interchangeable parts, complementary tools, multipurpose pieces, compactness, the links between form and function, etc.)

8. *Consider alternative metaphors.* To succeed in your profession, should you act more like a general, a religious leader, a mountain climber, or a competitive swimmer? If you're hiring a new employee, is the environment you're bringing the person into more like a family, a well-oiled machine, or an army? To succeed in the industry you're thinking of entering, should your company behave more like a football team, an orchestra, or like the parts of a Japanese garden? (Use of the garden metaphor has been credited with helping the Japanese focus on the long-term—like growing a tree.)

Male managers commonly use sports metaphors. They emphasize competition, team work, discipline, practice, designated roles, and a motivating team spirit. (Lee Iacocca's autobiography suggests he learned more management from Vince Lombardi than from anyone in the auto industry.)

But don't settle for thinking about your business in terms of just any sport. Think about *what kind* of athletic contest it most resembles. Citicorp, the far-flung financial-services company, likes to think of itself as a baseball team. (Baseball is a highly decentralized sport.) Caterpillar Tractor prefers metaphors from the centralized world of American football. Tandem computers, competing in the fast-moving world of high technology, uses the metaphor of basketball. The box on page 48 illustrates the contrasts between football and basketball as a framing metaphor. (It is based on the work of Robert W. Keidel.)

9. *Find out how the other guy does it.* Has someone else already solved a problem almost exactly like yours? Use the

47

DIFFERENT SPORTS, DIFFERENT FRAMES

A sports team is different from a family, a military unit, or a machine. But not all sports are alike. Robert W. Keidel has contrasted football, baseball, and basketball. For instance, the implications that follow from the football and basketball frames may be very different.

FOOTBALL	BASKETBALL
The emphasis is on	
Planning	Doing
Prepared strategy	Strategic adjustment
(the game plan)	(during the game)
The structure is	
Segmented units	Interaction among units
(offense, defense, special teams)	
Specific skills	General skills
(quarterback, center,	(all players pass, shoot,
punter, etc.)	play defense, rebound,
	etc.)
The flow of the game is characterized mainly by	
Set plays	Opportunism
(the play book, new	(take the best available
plays for a specific	action whenever the
game)	ball is obtained, e.g.,
	fast break vs. set play.)
Time segments	Continuous flow
(with planning between segments)	
Change and surprise are	Change and surprise are an
disruptive of the game	expected part of the
plan. Avoid them.	game. Take advantage
	of them.
The head coach is	
Sometimes a star himself,	Rarely as valuable and
as famous as the star	well known as the best
players.*	player.*
Unthinkable as a player-coach	Possibly a player-coach
(a planner, not a doer)	(though this occurs rarely)

*Can you name three current football coaches who are Hall of Fame material? Now, can you name three current basketball coaches who are Hall of Fame material (as coaches, not as players)?

Frame Discovery Worksheet below to abstract the essence of your problem and consider whether someone has already solved it for you. This is the approach we used with the advertising agency we mentioned in the introduction. Their problem was clients demanding lower commission rates. Abstractly summarized, that was: "Cut costs and increase revenue."

Other organizations, ranging from manufacturers of industrial products to universities, have used a process similar to this to discover the marketing frame that consumer products companies adopted after World War II. The abstract summary of their problem was: "Excess capacity." The solution was: Learn to understand potential buyers better.

10. *Monitor the changing world.* You can track frame shifts occurring in your industry or in the nation as a whole. How are people currently changing the way they frame important questions? Do they know something that your frame keeps you from perceiving?

Many important frame shifts are now taking place in American business. They may stimulate you to consider similar changes in your own frames:

Complaining Customers. In many companies, a customer who complains has long been viewed as either a simple pain in the neck or a potential litigant. The customer's claims would be denied almost automatically and probably handled by the legal department. Inspired by the Japanese, many American firms now view complaints as important *free* sources of information that will help them create more competitive products. Some firms (such as Procter & Gamble) provide toll-free numbers that customers can use to register complaints, and the comments are channeled systematically back to the design and manufacturing departments.

FRAME DISCOVERY WORKSHEET

Has Someone Else Solved Your Problem?

My problem

Abstract summary of my problem

The problem in their frame

Their solution

New ideas for my problem

One study of a variety of consumer products for which the potential loss to the consumer exceeded $100 estimated that 54 percent of consumers whose complaints were satisfactorily resolved repurchased the product, compared with 9 percent of unhappy customers who did not bother to complain. (Even those who complained and got an *unsatisfactory* response repurchased far more often than those who did not complain at all. Perhaps because talking to someone at the company who was interested in the problem persuaded them that the company cared about their welfare after all.)

Pollution. Many companies (about 80 percent according to one study) reacted to the pollution regulations of the 1970s by simply trapping and filtering emissions "at the end of the pipe." The pollution issue was framed: "How can we filter it out and get rid of it quickly?" Costs rose and operating efficiency declined. A few companies (such as 3M and Dow Corning) chose to reengineer products and manufacturing processes to recycle pollutants or avoid producing them—and this proved cheaper in the long run. Now pollution questions are more commonly framed: "What is the cheapest way to produce products with less pollution?"

Negotiation. Traditionally most negotiations were framed with the war or sports metaphor, in terms of "winning or losing." This zero-sum view is giving way to a "both-can-win" frame. Such popular books as *Getting to Yes* by Roger Fisher and William Ury frame negotiation more as a journey than as a battle. They argue that both parties can arrive at or near their goals. Some problems, such as salary negotiations, may seem truly zero-sum. But salary negotiations are only zero-sum if framed in short-run financial terms—not if such dimen-

51

sions as professional growth, recognition, responsibility, promotion, etc., are included.

Quality Control. For decades, U.S. companies felt they had achieved quality if they limited the number of reported defects to a few percent or a few "parts per thousand." Recently many have discovered that quality and reliability can improve essentially without limit, especially if products are designed "robustly"—to withstand the irreducible variations in manufacturing. At one company, ITT, the new frame led to fundamental redesign of an information systems product for greater simplicity. That one effort cut the defect rate in half and saved the company $60 million a year. Few of the techniques were really new; the key change was a reframing from seeking "acceptable" quality to seeking continuous improvement.

Selecting a Winning Frame

A winning decision **frame** captures more of the reality you are trying to manage without greatly increasing the complexity you have to deal with. If there is a golden rule of frame selection it is: *Fit the frame to the problem.* That sounds obvious, but few people manage to do it consistently. Why? First, because most people are unaware of their own frames and second, because they don't find more than one frame to pick from.

Some companies have been able to create a winning frame for their entire businesses. Schlumberger, the giant oil-field services company, began as a technology-driven seismic recording firm. It reframed its business as "providing information to the petroleum industry" and was able to grow to a $5

52

billion-plus, highly profitable company that way. IBM constantly reminded its people that, "IBM means service," and thereby articulated an aspect of business' needs in which it could clearly excel and create enormous value in an industry where attention flows naturally to technology, not service.

Strongly held frames, however, can also cause problems. One breakfast food company (realizing that people can eat only a finite amount of breakfast food) launched an exhaustive search for ways to profitably expand its product line. One product consistently offered the best opportunity: dog food. Yet executives rejected the dog food business because it didn't match their self-image. That company needs some soul-searching. It should either define just why the analysis that recommended entering the dog food business was wrong, or else expand the borders of its frame. But it should not lightly abandon a strong frame.

For each frame that now seems plausible to you, try to specify what is emphasized and what is minimized, concealed, distorted, or bounded out altogether. Try completing a Frame Analysis Worksheet (p. 45) for each of several possible frames. Then see which seems to throw most light on your issue.

Remember that you are as much an artist when you create and choose a problem frame as a scientist. Seek the frame through which the essence of the decision is best revealed.

If You Can't Choose a "Best" Frame, Find a Robust Solution

If you can find one frame that captures an entire situation better than any other, you should simply pick the best decision under that frame. You may even be able to depend on a quantitative model produced with a computer spreadsheet program or other quantitative decision-modeling tool. If you seek to invest in real estate for income, capital gains, and tax benefits, for example, you may be able to capture that decision in one complete frame.

In many cases, however, you won't find one frame clearly superior to others. If so, you should try using several frames, one after the other.

Consider the complex problem of valuing a company in an acquisition. At least four different approaches make sense:

1. **Net present value of the dividend stream:** i.e., expected cash flows discounted for risk and time.

2. **Liquidation value:** the cash equivalent of all assets if sold in an orderly fashion.

3. **Market value:** based on prices recently paid for similar companies.

4. **Stock value:** how much the firm is worth to its current owners as revealed by the price of its stock.

Important aspects may be left out of any of the four approaches. The only sensible way to decide what a company is worth is to try all four, and perhaps others besides, and look at how the results compare. In corporate acquisitions, moreover, a clear common denominator exists among the frames: dollars. You can calculate the firm's value under each approach and assume that you have a good chance of selling the company for the highest of the values you've calculated.

In many cases, however, plausible methods of framing complex problems possess no simple relationship to each other. One way of approaching the problem may yield a description that in some ways complements but in others seems to contradict the results of other equally plausible approaches.

When this happens, make sure your business chooses a robust solution. In other words, search for a solution that points toward success under several different approaches.

The Parable of the Kitchen Spindle

The wonderful Parable of the Kitchen Spindle (first published in the *Harvard Business Review* in 1962) illustrates the power of frames and the idea of robust solutions:

> A restaurant owner found his cooks and waitresses were bickering about orders, especially during peak hours. He consulted four specialists, representing four different disciplines:
>
> > A *sociologist* framed the problem in terms of status and hierarchy: the cooks resented receiving orders from the lower status waitresses. He recommended sensitivity training for both the cooks and the waitresses.
> >
> > An *anthropologist* stressed cultural norms, especially concerning sex roles. The male cooks disliked having their actions initiated by women. He recommended that a senior cook be given authority to manage the system—he could tell the waitresses where to leave their orders and parcel them out among the cooks.
> >
> > A *psychologist* diagnosed the problem in terms of sibling rivalry: the cooks and the waitresses were like brothers and sisters competing for approval of the boss, who had become a parent figure to them. He recommended weekly counseling sessions for both groups to improve communication.
> >
> > An *information theorist* blamed "cognitive overload." At peak times, too many orders had to be memorized, resulting in tension and friction around the kitchen. He

recommended waitresses punch the orders into a new computer system, which would display the right orders at the right time for each cook.

The manager was thoroughly confused. He feared he could not afford any of these solutions. What if he invested in one of them and it did not work? In desperation, he mentioned the problem to a junior cook. "You know, in the restaurant where I used to work they had a rotating thing in the kitchen and we clipped our orders to it," he replied. "The cooks could just turn it around and pull off an order each time they were ready to start cooking something new. It made everything a lot easier. Do you think that would work here?"

The boss said he didn't know. So he took the idea back to the four experts. Each continued to recommend the course of action first proposed, but each also said the kitchen spindle might help alleviate the problem:

The sociologist said the spindle would align statuses (since the orders would have to wait until the cook got them).

The anthropologist said the spindle would impersonalize the initiation of action, thereby freeing the cooks from the despised reversal of sex roles.

The psychologist said the spindle would reduce the friction-causing interaction between cook and waitress, minimizing sibling rivalry.

The information theorist said the spindle would give the system external memory comparable to a computer's (i.e., the orders would be saved on paper).

The boss installed the kitchen spindle, and it was a smashing success. He never had to consider any of the experts' other advice further.

The moral, of course, is that when a decision makes sense through several different frames, it is probably a good decision.

Robust Solutions in the Real World

Some companies have developed extensive systems that force them to find robust solutions. In strategic planning, for instance, a company could ask managers to develop several scenarios or thinking frames for the future and ask how well their current strategies would hold up under each of the scenarios. This stimulates a search for an option acceptable under multiple scenarios or frames. Such choices may be far better bets than those that merely promise optimum success under conditions that managers believe are the "most likely" future developments (i.e., a single frame).

Royal Dutch/Shell, for instance, has developed an elaborate system of scenario planning so as to look at the world through multiple windows. The strategic planning department (in London) might present operating managers with:

—one scenario that describes the future the corporate planners consider "surprise-free"—say, slow but steady economic growth and stable oil prices;

—one scenario that describes a future of international shocks due to revolutions in oil-producing nations, low economic growth, and high, volatile oil prices;

—one scenario that describes a future of high economic growth with low oil prices due to intensive energy conservation and rapid technological progress;

etc.

Shell usually restricts the number of scenarios to a minimum of two and a maximum of four. Each, however, must be plausible and internally consistent. Shell then makes strategic decisions based on their likely impact under each of the scenarios. For instance, investments in new gas stations might be highly profitable under the scenario the corporation's economists consider most likely. But they might be unprofitable under *both* a low economic growth scenario (because consumers would be driving less) *and* a technology-driven high-growth scenario (because changes in automobiles might make them use less gas and require fewer repairs).

On the other hand, investment in an efficient new refinery might make sense under all three scenarios: It might produce increased sales under the moderate and high-growth scenarios, and also help the corporation cut costs under the low-growth scenario.

Shell has greatly benefited from this approach. It has consistently anticipated price drops better than other oil companies, and it coped with the overcapacity in oil shipping in the early 1980s far better than its rivals. Industry analysts consider it one of the best-managed oil companies. (We'll discuss concrete steps in creating a scenario in Chapter 5.)

Framing: A Top Management Job

The higher a person rises in an organization, the more time should be spent on framing issues. In a complex and uncertain world, senior managers can't be expected to always choose the alternative that in hindsight produces the best possible outcome. But good senior managers can be expected to ensure that:

—the entire organization frames questions thoughtfully,

—the dominant frames used throughout the organization are appropriate, and

58

—complex decisions are evaluated through a variety of alternative frames.

Managers must address the framing issue even before they've chosen someone to study it. Whoever drafts a report or even an agenda starts to frame the problem—thus senior managers need to provide framing guidance even at this stage. They can either assign the frame to the subordinate or work with the subordinate to choose a frame that both find productive.

Frame Misalignment Prevents Communication

Understanding frames also helps you communicate with others and convince them to do what you want.

People often fail to convince others because their frame differs from their listener's frame. The two have simplified the world in different ways, and the talker can't communicate through the simplification the listener uses. Consider the following example:

The biotechnology firm Genentech was shocked in May 1987 when the Food and Drug Administration panel refused to approve its anti-clotting drug tPA. The company had been so certain the drug would be approved that it had already invested hundreds of millions of dollars in plant and equipment to produce the new drug, employed hundreds of people in preparing the product for market, launched an advertising campaign touting its impending availability, and built up a large inventory of the drug that would deteriorate within two years if it could not be sold.

Genentech's leaders included biochemists and molecular biologists whose frame emphasized the reliability of evidence from controlled laboratory tests. In preparation for the FDA

59

panel meeting, Genentech had produced reams of laboratory evidence that tPA could dissolve and reduce the formation of blood clots.

But the FDA panel consisted largely of medical specialists whose frame emphasized the importance of *clinical* evidence. They wanted to see evidence based on the actual treatment of patients (i.e., a clinical frame). They knew a great deal about how the real world could differ from the laboratory, and they had limited faith in the scientific reasons Genentech advanced that their laboratory tests, unlike some others in medical history, reliably demonstrated the efficacy of their drug.

Genentech had prepared relatively little clinical evidence, and placed little emphasis on the clinical evidence that it had. Within a week after the drug was rejected, Genentech's stock dropped 24 percent—almost a billion dollars in market value.

How to Communicate Better by Understanding Frames

Good communicators align their message with their listeners' frames. When encyclopedia salespeople knock on your door, for example, they look for aspects of your life that both of you share, and talk about them to demonstrate that their thinking is compatible with yours and therefore trustworthy.

Consider a small consulting firm that had to align its frame when a Caribbean resort hired it to cut costs. The consultants found an efficiently run resort that was ignoring important segments to make more money. The resort focused its marketing exclusively on a small, traditional clientele. It neglected convention business and joint reservation and marketing opportunities with other resorts.

The consultants saw the missed chances as "opportunity costs"—costs of forgone opportunities. Opportunity costs can rarely be directly measured, but the consultants' frame—wisely—treated them equal in importance to outright waste. Thus the consultants told the resort's management that they should be attacked as aggressively as out-of-pocket costs, and urged a new approach to marketing.

The manager, a self-made man, couldn't see their point. He cared about eliminating what he saw to be waste currently taking place, not the new opportunities envisaged by the consultants.

Finally, the consultants thought of a way to switch the manager's reference point from current revenues to what revenue *would be* if the right opportunities were seized. "By not taking these actions," they said, "you are losing $78 million a year."

Later, the consultants admitted to us that the $78 million statistic was "speculative" to say the least. But making up a number was well justified. "It was the only way we could get through to them," they said.

Knowing your listener's frame is essential in communicating with anyone. When you need to convince someone, you can often align yourself by role-playing your listeners in advance. You may also want to fill out a Frame Analysis Worksheet as illustrated on page 45 to try to pin down their frame in detail.

Understanding Frames in Negotiations

In negotiations, understanding your opposite's frame can allow you to achieve great success. Many auto dealers, for instance, frame their sales strategies using a technique they call "four square." They try to determine how the customer frames the purchase:

—some emphasize minimizing the bottom-line price of the car;

—some emphasize minimizing monthly payments;

—some emphasize maximizing the trade-in allowance on their old car;

—some emphasize minimizing the down payment.

After determining how the customer frames the problem, dealers use that knowledge to pack their markup into the parts of the transaction that are in the shadows of the buyer's frame.

A few buyers use a knowledge of the four-square frame to trick dealers into giving them spectacular deals. For example, Ken Carpenter makes his living selling supplies to Oregon automobile dealers and has many friends among them. Once, he says, a dealer tricked him into a bet on which he lost $370.

At three o'clock on the last Saturday afternoon of the month, "I knew that dealer wouldn't be in, that the salesmen would be tired, and that they would be anxious to meet their monthly quotas," Carpenter recalls. He sought out a rookie salesman, suggested he intended to make a large down payment and finance the rest, and kept pushing to minimize the difference between the down payment and the final cost. The salesman could expect to make a profit on financing and add-ons such as credit life insurance. Following the dealership's customary procedure for tough customers, the rookie passed Carpenter on to the senior salesperson on floor duty, who in turn passed him on to the sales manager for the entire dealership. The sales manager agreed on the price Carpenter wanted—just a few dollars over the dealer's cost. But he indicated a monthly payment that implied a high finance rate. Then he passed Carpenter on to the finance and insurance office, where he presumed the dealership would earn its profit.

In the finance office, Carpenter refused all financing terms and add-ons offered, and wrote out a check for the full

62

difference between the agreed-upon down payment and the total price of the car.

With relish, Carpenter remembers: "The dealer came in on Monday morning and threw a living fit when he found out what I had done. He called me. When I asked him, 'Did I get you for more than $370?' the dealer slammed down the phone. We're still friends, though."

Framing Your Decisions: Conclusions

Controlling the frame of a decision can be a source of both power and wisdom. Making decisions through inferior frames—or with no well-organized frames at all—eventually leads to disaster.

Frame control demands that every major decision include at least four steps:

1. Identify the frame you or your organization would automatically (and often unthinkingly) use.

2. Find one or more reasonable alternative frames.

3. Analyze where each frame fits and what it distorts or leaves out of bounds.

4. Match the frame to the problem, i.e., choose from the alternative frames the one (or ones) that you consider most appropriate.

If one single frame captures the problem's essence, run with it. You are like an artist who has created a masterpiece.

If no such single frame exists, you need to look at the problem through several frames to find a robust solution.

Either route gives you an excellent chance for success.

Part II

INFORMATION-GATHERING AND INTELLIGENCE

Chapter 4
Knowing What You Don't Know

That idea is so damned nonsensical and impossible that I'm willing to stand on the bridge of a battleship while that nitwit tries to hit it from the air.

NEWTON BAKER
*U.S. Secretary of War in 1921,
reacting to Brigadier General Billy Mitchell's
claim that airplanes could sink battleships by
dropping bombs on them.*

Newton Baker was one of the most remarkable men ever to serve as U.S. Secretary of War. He was an avowed pacifist when he took the post in 1916. (President Woodrow Wilson admired him because he had reformed Cleveland as city solicitor and mayor.) Congress, where Wilson's Democrats were a minority, denounced the "reforms" that pacifist Baker instituted. Yet after the United States entered World War I, Baker's dedication and spirit—and the efficiency of his department— won the respect of even Republicans.

How could a man of such caliber conclude he'd be perfectly safe standing on the bridge of a battleship while the country's best pilots attacked it with bombs? The most obvious answer is that Baker and his War Department made an error in judgment. That can happen to even the best decision-makers. Many educated people in the World War I era believed that no gnat of an airplane could sink a battleship.

But the main error was much worse than guessing wrong: Baker's big mistake was holding his beliefs with utter conviction, without considering whether the available information justified the depth of that conviction. Baker knew with total— and totally unjustified—certainty that planes could not sink ships.

An open-minded review should have shown Baker that he had no grounds to be so certain. And he should have ordered a test.

When Warren Harding succeeded Wilson, General Mitchell's squadron of tiny planes got a chance to demonstrate its power. They promptly turned a supposedly unsinkable dreadnought into a permanent part of the ocean floor. (Baker had returned to Cleveland and resumed a successful law practice, so he did not stand on the bridge during the assault.)

Baker's error illustrates the mistakes intelligent people can commit when they fail to evaluate carefully the information they possess.

It also illustrates two more decision traps common to most of humankind.

Decision Trap Number 4:

Overconfidence in Your Judgment—Failing to collect key factual information because you are too sure of your assumptions and opinions.

Decision Trap Number 5:

Shortsighted Shortcuts—Relying inappropriately on "rules of thumb" such as implicitly trusting the most readily available information or anchoring too much on convenient facts.

These dangers can cause problems throughout the decision-making process, but they particularly affect the gathering of information and intelligence. Wise decision-makers, avoid them and work to assure high-quality intelligence. They explicitly list what information is needed to make the decision well. They stop early in the decision process to inventory the intelligence already available. Finally, they constantly remember the threats of overconfidence, the availability bias, and the anchoring trap.

Sizing Up What You Know

Sometimes the process of framing your decision forces you to list all the information you need. If you're choosing a law firm, for example, assembling the yardsticks of your frame may lead naturally to the questions you want to ask the firms you will consider.

If you haven't listed the information you want during framing, do that as soon as you have a frame you're happy with. Make your list without regard to how difficult acquiring the information might be. Feel free to list information that might seem impossible to obtain ("the inflation rate five years from now"). The intelligence-gathering portion of the decision process includes not just the gathering of hard information, but all the elements that the military includes under the heading "intelligence"—such as ballpark estimates or guesses regarding key questions about which exact information can't be found. It is difficult to make really good estimates of what is only partly known. Yet, this is often vital to an excellent decision.

Collecting information and using it *systematically* will reduce the dangers from overconfidence, availability bias, and anchoring. But guarding against these errors also demands a sophisticated appreciation of how and *why* they affect bright people, and sometimes it demands the use of special methods or techniques.

Overconfidence

Are you overconfident about what you believe? Dozens of studies have demonstrated that virtually all people put too much trust in their opinions. People "know" that certain steps are needed to solve their company's problems, etc. Indeed, many people suffer from overconfidence in what they *believe* even if their belief entails a negative view of their own worth and abilities. Insecure people are much more certain that they are inadequate than any real evidence justifies!

If you doubt you suffer from overconfidence in your judgment, try the following test. It contains ten trivia questions, and you can do well on the test without knowing the actual answers for any of them. All we ask is that for each question, you provide a high and a low estimate. Choose your estimates for each question so that you are 90 percent confident that the true answer is within the range you're providing. In other words, aim to provide ranges wide enough so that only one of the ten answers is outside your ranges. Note that we are not interested in this test in how much you know about trivia, but rather in how well you know what you *don't know*. What you know about history or geography may or may not matter in your life, but what you know about yourself—about your own knowledge—matters a great deal. This quiz reveals whether you tend to overestimate your knowledge.

Did you get more than one wrong? If so, you are not alone. In our experience with over 1,000 American and European managers, less than 1 percent had either zero or one miss out of ten questions. Most managers missed four to seven out of ten. They thought their knowledge was much better than it really was.

Might you be overconfident on our trivia test, but estimate accurately in your regular work? You might, and we'll suggest some techniques in the next chapter that might help you to do so. But our own studies, using industry and job-specific questions, show most people do not.

The following table shows that overconfidence strikes in a broad range of tasks. The Harvard MBAs answered questions similar to our trivia test, except that they were asked to put down ranges about which they were 98 percent sure—so for only 2 percent of the questions should the correct answer have fallen outside their ranges. In fact it fell outside 46 percent of the time. (Unfortunately, our own MBA students at Chicago and Cornell don't do any better.)

Even chemical-industry managers, when given company- and industry-specific questions, exhibit striking overconfidence. When they were asked for 90 percent confidence ranges, so that they should have only 10 percent misses, the true answer lay outside their ranges 50 percent of the time. Thus they came a bit closer than the students, but they were still grossly overconfident. Indeed, even when asked to give 50 percent confidence ranges—in other words, ranges for which the odds were even that the true answer was inside or outside their range—managers couldn't do it. They missed their mark about two-thirds of the time.

RESULTS OF OVERCONFIDENCE TESTS

Type of People Tested	Type of Question Asked	PERCENTAGE OF MISSES Ideal Target	Actually Observed
Harvard MBA's	Trivia facts	2%	46%
Employees of a chemical company	Chemical industry and company-specific facts	10% 50%	50% 79%
Managers of a computer co.	General business facts Company-specific facts	5% 5%	80% 58%
Physicians	Probability that a patient has pneumonia	0-20%	82%
Physicists	Scientific estimates like the speed of light	32%	41%

Other professions are afflicted as well.

Physicians diagnosing for pneumonia erred as badly as managers. Indeed, even scientists, using quantitative models and statistical error theory, were slightly overconfident.

The problem persists in the heart of business. One manager at a Fortune 500 company studied company files for information on the completion times of more than eighty projects. He obtained the original estimates of completion times (in person-days) and compared them with the times actually taken. Sometimes the estimates were correct: For projects where the firm had directly comparable experience, actual completion times averaged 3 percent less than estimates. But when the firm tried to do something new, it almost always suffered from overconfidence about how quickly it could do the work. Completion times averaged 18 percent above the original estimate, and too often fell outside people's confidence ranges.

Decision Trap Number 4:

Overconfidence in Your Judgment—Failing to collect key factual information because you are too sure of your assumptions and opinions.

Among "experts," overconfidence leads to statements like that of Newton Baker and others listed in the box on page 74. Take a few seconds to study the list. Many "experts" who speak overconfidently will suffer little. Often their incomes do not depend on being right; they just depend on "speaking with authority." But in business, overconfidence usually leads to wrong decisions, shrinking profit margins, firings, or bankruptcies.

OVERCONFIDENCE AMONG EXPERTS

Heavier-than-air flying machines are impossible.
LORD KELVIN—*British mathematician, physicist, and president of the British Royal Society, c. 1895.*

Reagan doesn't have the presidential look.
UNITED ARTISTS EXECUTIVE—*dismissing the idea that Ronald Reagan be offered the starring role in the movie* THE BEST MAN, 1964.

A severe depression like that of 1920–21 is outside the range of probability.
HARVARD ECONOMIC SOCIETY—*Weekly Letter* November 16, 1929

We know on the authority of Moses, that longer ago than six thousand years, the world did not exist.
MARTIN LUTHER—*1483–1546; German leader of the Protestant Reformation.*

Impossible!
JIMMY "THE GREEK" SNYDER—*odds maker, when asked whether he thought Cassius Clay could last six rounds in his upcoming bout with World Heavyweight Champion Sonny Liston, 1964.*

They couldn't hit an elephant at this dist___
GENERAL JOHN B. SEDGWICK—*Union Army Civil War officer's last words, uttered during the Battle of Spotsylvania, 1864.*

Overconfidence often strikes whole organizations. In his book *Groupthink*, Irving Janis reviews well-known fiascoes like the Japanese attack on Pearl Harbor, the bugging of Democratic headquarters in the Watergate Hotel in Washington, D.C., and United States conduct in the Vietnam War. Janis found that many could be traced to overconfidence pervading organizations.

Corporations seem to perform only slightly better than governments. Think of Genentech's hundreds of millions of dollars invested in manufacturing the unapproved tPA (mentioned in the last chapter). Think of Ford's Edsel. (The company halted market research two years before the product's introduction because it was afraid that researchers working with the public would let information about Ford's "great idea" leak out.) Think of Chicago's Continental Bank. (It "knew" that energy loans were secure because the price of oil could do nothing but rise.)

Confirmation Bias

Overconfidence is related to another problem: People's fondness for evidence that will confirm, rather than challenge, their current beliefs.

Most of us seem to possess a built-in tendency to favor data that support our current beliefs and to dismiss evidence that upsets them. This can lead large organizations far off-course because often a diligent search can turn up hundreds of pieces of evidence that seem to confirm a hypothesis even though the hypothesis isn't true.

James R. Emshoff and Ian I. Mitroff, two professors working at the Wharton Applied Research Center in the mid 1970s, studied strategy formulation in America's largest companies. In dozens of companies, they found well-paid executives

75

simply using the latest sophisticated computer information systems to produce data supporting the strategies they had already decided to adopt. Many of the strategies failed miserably for reasons that should have been predictable with or without the computers. "The key issue isn't getting the right facts but challenging the right assumptions," they noted.

Most of us favor confirming evidence even when the search for confirming evidence has clearly become unhelpful. Confirming evidence gives us a mental reward. Every shred says: "You're on the right track. . . . You're doing a good job."

Disconfirming evidence, on the other hand, says: "Your idea wasn't as good as you thought." In short, confirmation feels good and disconfirmation feels (at least momentarily) painful. Thus people tend to neglect evidence that might undermine their ideas.

Moral: *Have the discipline to seek information that might disconfirm your opinions*. If you look for it and can't find it, *then* you have reason to be confident. One way to look for it is to generate an alternative hypothesis and test both.

Know What You Don't Know

Explicitly developing a frame for your decision is a partial antidote to overconfidence in your judgment. Carefully defining the question usually helps you appreciate its difficulty. Clearly listing the intelligence needed for a decision is a further weapon against overconfidence, and so is a recognition of our innate bias to favor evidence that confirms our views.

Ultimately, however, avoiding overconfidence means developing good secondary knowledge—having a good understanding of what you know and what you don't know.

Primary knowledge consists of facts and principles we believe are true. The historical facts of the Great Depression, the knowledge that a game of basketball can produce a pulled muscle, and an appreciation of the strength of steel—all fall into the category of primary knowledge.

General Mitchell used primary knowledge to predict that planes could sink battleships. He knew that airplanes could drop bombs, and that battleships could not dodge them. Newton Baker used primary knowledge, too. He knew the strength of steel and the difficulty of hitting a moving target from a rapidly moving airplane. But Newton Baker lacked secondary knowledge—an awareness of how reliable his primary knowledge was for predicting the destructive power of an airplane carrying bombs.

Primary knowledge determines the direction of our opinion; secondary knowledge should determine our confidence. You need to develop your secondary knowledge. And you need to cultivate subordinates and advisers with good secondary knowledge.

Don't Listen to Ned Knowall

Consider two individuals: Ned Knowall and Mel Meek. Both have some expertise (say, in tax law). You must rely on one of them for advice.

Mr. Knowall knows more; his primary knowledge surpasses Mr. Meek's. He would do better than Mr. Meek on any true-false test about his field. But unfortunately Mr. Knowall believes that he has even more knowledge than he actually possesses. Sometimes he has assured you that a tax move was impossible when, in fact, it turned out that you could have done what you wanted. Mr. Meek, in contrast, appreciates what he does not know. He will do research or ask for help when unsure of an answer. On the true-false test, Mr. Meek would know he was often guessing.

77

Which adviser should you prefer? Most of the time Mr. Meek will turn out to be the better choice. To gather intelligence successfully, we must clearly know the limits of our knowledge. If Mr. Knowall promises that he knows all about depreciation law and then he misses a crucial angle, your company could lose millions.

So who would you hire? Unfortunately, Westerners will probably choose Mr. Knowall. We associate confidence with competence. So our culture encourages overconfidence.

People like Mr. Knowall even fool the Supreme Court, which has stated that an eyewitness's level of confidence is one of the factors judges and juries should use to assess the truth of testimony. In U.S. courts, credibility often depends on how certain a witness claims to be. Indeed, lawyers work hard to make clear to a jury that the witness is certain, repeatedly asking, "Are you positive?"

However, here the U.S. judicial system errs. Greater confidence does not necessarily mean greater accuracy. In one early study, psychologist William Stern showed three simple pictures to thirty well-educated adults. They sat down immediately to write down what they had seen, underlining the parts that they would swear to. Of the sixty-three statements that subjects were willing to take an oath on, fifty contained errors.

In a more recent study, on a scale where 0 represented no relation between accuracy and confidence and 100 represented complete agreement, the average correlation was only 7. In other words, the correlation between confidence and accuracy was virtually nonexistent. Jurors would judge accuracy better if they focus on whether testimony jibes with other evidence, rather than on how deeply the witness seems to believe it.

Overconfidence as a Strategic Weapon

Many managers in our seminars don't like the idea that they should fight overconfidence. They say: "I need to feel confident to work well."

Why do people need confidence so badly? Is it ever right to be truly overconfident?

Actually, there is a place for overconfidence in the book of effective tactics. When "positive thinking" is used deliberately and strategically, it can yield excellent results. It can help you land a sales contract or persuade top management to approve a proposal.

The ideal business person is a *realist* when making a decision but an *optimist* when implementing it. Unfortunately, few people can switch between realism and optimism at exactly the right time. To be effective, you have to motivate subordinates by convincing them that something is achievable—without developing an unrealistic belief in it yourself.

How do you maintain your detached decision-making ability, yet motivate your people effectively? Look at how great generals have led their troops. They manage reports to the foot soldiers in an optimistic way. But they try to avoid all distortions in their planning. They ask tough questions. They seek the real truth.

Once they decide on a plan of battle and head out to the campground to rally the troops, however, they radiate confidence.

In a corporation, as in an army, a strategic dose of overconfidence can motivate the doers, but the planners should maintain a realistic attitude. This sounds simple, at an abstract level. But where does the shift from deciders to doers actually occur? Many people play both roles.

79

The bottom line is that *overconfidence needs to be under-stood and managed*, both within the organization and within ourselves. Good secondary knowledge must be combined with an instinct for when "positive thinking" is valuable (and not too dangerous!).

Managing overconfidence means that when you gather intelligence or make a decision, you should be careful to think in a realistic mode. Consider your options, specify ranges or probabilities, and weigh the possibilities—downside as well as up.

But when the time comes to implement the decision, think positive. Go all out for success (within realism). Persuade others to get on board, to work enthusiastically. When you put overconfidence to work for you in this way, then you are managing it.

In essence, overconfidence is a two-edged sword, entailing the following dilemma:

> *To know that we know what we know, and that we do not know what we do not know, that is true knowledge.*
>
> CONFUCIUS
>
> *For a man to achieve all that is demanded of him, he must regard himself as greater than he is.*
>
> GOETHE

We agree with Goethe when it comes to implementation. But we prefer Confucius at the moment of decision.

"Rules of Thumb": The Need and the Dangers

In addition to overconfidence, you have to watch out for decision-making shortcuts you use instinctively but don't fully understand. They can involve quite separate problems.

We all need decision-making shortcuts just as we need

80

decision frames. Without "rules of thumb," we could never make all the estimates and choices we must make in daily life. For example, you may have a rule of thumb that says you will delegate attendance at interdepartmental budget meetings to your subordinate unless you hear that a crucial item is on the agenda. The only alternative to using this kind of rule of thumb is to carefully study the question of when you will attend interdepartmental budget meetings, collect information about the agenda of each one, and then make a well-thought-out decision. No one can—or should even try to—make that kind of careful decision on every question.

Technically rules of thumb and similar decision-making shortcuts are called heuristics. The term comes from the Greek word for "discover." Heuristics are mental procedures designed to cut out a lot of effort and yet still arrive at the right answer or a close approximation.

Rules of thumb and other heuristics greatly ease the judgment process. You don't even realize what rules of thumb you are using much of the time. You follow at least some implicit rules without knowing you are using them.

Unfortunately, that can get you into trouble. You may continue to use a good rule of thumb when you've moved to a question where it is inappropriate. Your rules of thumb— even those learned in advanced courses in universities—are potential hazards, not guarantees of success.

Misleading shortcuts give people false intelligence, and can derail the entire decision process. We next discuss two of the most dangerous mental shortcuts in information-gathering and intelligence. They are (1) the tendency to *pay too much attention to the most readily available information* and (2) the tendency to excessively *anchor* opinions in a single statistic or fact that from then on dominates the thinking process.

The Available Data Aren't Always the Best

People seem to implicitly assume that *the information that is most easily available to them is also the most relevant information*. They often fail even to think through the possible implications of information that would be harder to get. Psychologists call this the availability bias.

To illustrate how availability can bias our intelligence, try the following quiz. Below are pairs of causes of death:

> Pair 1: Lung Cancer vs. Motor Vehicle Accidents
> Pair 2: Emphysema vs. Homicide
> Pair 3: Tuberculosis vs. Fire and Flames

From each pair, choose the one you think causes more deaths in the United States each year.

We have shown these pairs to many people, including numerous managers. Invariably the majority selects the second item in each pair.

Before looking at the correct answers, consider how you arrived at your judgments. Did you select your answer to the first question by asking yourself, "How often have I heard of people dying from lung cancer versus being killed in automobile accidents?" Probably not consciously. But your impressions presumably developed from the instances of lung cancer and car crashes that you had heard about. If your impression was that you had heard of more instances of auto accidents than of lung cancer, then you chose accidents.

This kind of judgment process is reasonable much of the time. However, how well does the frequency with which we hear about accidents mirror the frequency of their actual occurrence? We learn of fatalities mostly through the news media, which report events on the basis of their "newswor-

82

thiness" rather than the true frequency of occurrence. Death from lung cancer is not considered newsworthy unless the person is well known. In contrast, a motor vehicle death is routinely considered "news."

The following table shows survey results for each pair, and also lists the frequency with which two typical newspapers published stories on each during a one-year period.

Cause of Death	People's Choice in Each Pair	Annual U.S. Total (in 1,000s)	Newspaper Reports Per Year
Lung Cancer	43%	140	3
Motor Vehicle Accidents	57%	46	127
Emphysema	45%	22	1
Homicide	55%	19	264
Tuberculosis	23%	4	0
Fire and Flames	77%	7	24

People do instinctively realize that they can fall victim to the availability bias. They know that they base some judgments on evidence that comes most easily to mind. And they also know that television, newspapers, and other readily available information sources can create skewed perspectives on reality. However, few put these two realizations together when making important judgments.

Consider how the availability heuristic may be affecting your professional judgments. Suppose that you must select either John or Frank to fill a new position. Many bosses just sit back and recall prior experiences with each employee. Suppose that you can remember several more outstanding achievements for John than for Frank, and you remember no serious problems with either one. The greater availability of favorable experiences might lead you to recommend John over Frank, especially if you're trying to decide quickly, without a comprehensive review.

But bosses who do this may fall victim to clever employees' strategic exploitation of the availability heuristic. Suppose that John simply set out to present his achievements to you in a highly memorable fashion, so that they could be more easily recalled in the future. He might "remind" you of accomplishments in memos or solicit positive letters from associates. Indeed, many "self-help" books advise people to behave this way. One common piece of advice is: "Deliver bad news orally and good news in writing."

Would this qualify John for the promotion more than Frank? Probably not. So the right way to choose who gets promoted is to first establish a frame for the decision: What evidence really would demonstrate who would perform the new job better? Then, rigorously list the available information. You could call this an intelligence audit. Finally, collect more information if you're not sufficiently confident about making the decision on the basis of the information at hand. Interview others who work with Frank and John. Don't let overconfidence or a subordinate exploiting the availability heuristic trap you into a decision that could profoundly harm your own career as well as that of a deserving employee.

Decision Trap Number 5:

Shortsighted Shortcuts—Relying inappropriately on "rules of thumb" such as implicitly trusting the most readily available information or anchoring too much on convenient facts.

Bias in Favor of Recent Evidence

Availability biases come in several varieties. One is the "recency effect." Every March, the Internal Revenue Service indicts some highly visible individuals for tax evasion. The IRS believes that recent newspaper articles about the agency's powers will make the dangers of income tax cheating more memorable when people file their returns in April.

The IRS's use of the recency effect is part of a strategy to achieve a positive end. But often the recency effect undermines business decisions. For example, one bank found its sales force constantly favored whatever products were most recently described in sales training sessions. A division of the bank marketed about thirty information services and reporting systems. But rather than choosing from the entire portfolio of products and recommending those truly appropriate to customer needs, sales people too often suggested the products about which they had most recently been trained. Sales calls were wasted.

By understanding the recency bias, you can often improve decision-making dramatically, however. When one of the bank's managers discovered this bias after hearing us lecture, the bank modified its sales training to ensure that each seminar concluded with a description of how the product under discussion fit into the bank's overall product line. And it produced a pamphlet that could be used to consistently remind the sales force about all the available products and the types of customers that each could best serve. Sales calls became better focused.

The recency effect can also mislead troubleshooters. In one case, whenever a large chemical company received a customer complaint about its industrial solvents, a technical specialist (typically a chemical engineer) analyzed the problem and rendered a diagnosis. Often, the expert diagnosed incorrectly. A new diagnosis had to be made. This continued until an adequate solution was found.

The company's quality control manager suspected that an availability bias was causing inaccurate diagnoses. He devised a test. He presented each of these experienced engineers with five solvent complaints, along with a list of plausible causes. He asked the engineers to assign a probability to each of the causes. He reviewed the answers along with the recent experience of each engineer.

Those who had recently experienced a particular cause deemed it much more likely—by a factor of anywhere from 15 to 50 percent. In other words, the engineers tended to pick as a problem's most likely cause the one they had most recently encountered in real life. The manager estimated that the company and its customers were losing about $2.6 million a year because recency effects were biasing problem diagnoses. He and his engineers analyzed past experience and prepared a guide to the actual probabilities of any particular cause producing particular symptoms. "My people are superbly trained chemical engineers," he admitted later, "but they've never been trained in making judgments."

Vividness

Vividness can also create an availability bias, and it's particularly hard to overcome. A single, vivid experience easily alters people's perceptions because it remains highly memorable and, therefore, highly available to the mind.

After a horror movie, people become frightened by shadows. After the media vividly document a catastrophic plane crash, people are afraid to fly. Remember your uneasiness at the beach the summer after you first saw the movie *Jaws*?

Lawyers now bring vividness into courtrooms by producing elaborate videotape documentaries in addition to traditional testimony. These videos reconstruct the accident or depict the daily struggle of the victim. Should they be admissible? Judges wrestling with that question should ask· Does the video bring the jury closer to or push it further from the true state of affairs?

Vivedness can interfere with business decisions. The pleasure of being wined and dined by a possible new supplier is more vivid than dry reliability statistics. We may know it exerts undue influence upon our perceptions. Yet we cannot overcome or suppress it fully. The best defense is a carefully drawn frame for the decision and careful efforts to improve aspects of your intelligence that may be weak.

One California company, Concord Capital Management of San Mateo, has explicitly targeted the area of heuristic biases as a promising avenue to outperforming the stock market. And so far—based on five years of published results—with considerable success. One of their strategies zeroed in on companies that were in the shadow of high visibility, "hit" companies with blockbuster products in either the movie or the toy industry. Such recent winners receive highly vivid coverage and lots of hype at the expense of the less fortunate—but perhaps equally capable firms. Investing in the presumed "losers" turned in a handsome profit, according to Concord founder Harold Arbit.

Does Your Anchor Hold You Back?

Anchoring, a common shortcut used especially when people need to make an estimate, creates additional problems in intelligence-gathering and decision-making. Suppose you are trying to decide whether to enter the widget business. You need to estimate the size of the market for widgets five years from now, or the appropriate salary for a plant manager.

Most people, consciously or unconsciously, start with a number that easily comes to mind—say, the number of widgets sold last year or the salary of your current manufacturing supervisor. Then they adjust up or down to reflect other significant facts.

This procedure seems sensible, but it suffers from a major defect: *people usually adjust insufficiently*. The initial number (i.e., the anchor) powerfully affects the analyst's mind and keeps the final judgment from moving as far as it should.

Anchors often contain useful information. If a natural anchor exists (last year's widget sales may be an example), it should not be disregarded. But the problem is that we often allow the anchor to exert too strong a hold.

Some Anchoring Experiments

To demonstrate the effect of anchoring on professionals, we performed the following experiment. First, we asked nearly 100 managers: "What is your best estimate of the prime interest rate six months from now?" Their average guess (and this was in 1983 when the real prime was around 11 percent) was 10.9 percent. This unanchored question serves as a control group.

Then we surveyed a second group with these two questions:

1. Do you believe that six months from now the prime rate will be above or below 8 percent? and

2. What is your best estimate of the prime rate six months from now?

We wanted to see if the first question, designed to anchor subjects on 8 percent, would "drag" estimates below those of the unanchored group. It did. The average guess was now 10.5 percent, or 40 basis points below the unanchored group. When we anchored a third group at 14 percent ("Do you believe that six months from now the prime rate will be above or below 14 percent?"), their average estimate was 11.2 percent.

Note how subtle anchoring can be. We didn't even tell participants we thought 8 percent and 14 percent were reasonable guesses. Many information sources with an interest in the outcome of your decision will use this kind of **strategic anchoring**—mention of a statistic to encourage the listener to anchor on it—to influence decision-makers' perception of the issues. Consider negotiations with a banker, for example. We know one lender who, when he wants to write a loan agreement at .5 percent above the prime rate, might say, "Generally we charge companies like yours 2 percent over prime." This high anchor allows him to "surrender" more than a full percentage point and still meet his initial target.

This common reframing tactic works well in negotiations when the initial anchor appears reasonable. So in many negotiations, the crucial issue is whose anchor will be accepted as the appropriate reference point. In one study with real estate agents, it was found that using different anchors (in the form of high versus low listing prices) caused differences in the "independent" appraisals on the order of 9 percent of the home's value.

Irrelevant Anchors

Do interest rate anchors work just because listeners assume that the person offering the anchor knows something they don't? In other words, does the anchor drag the estimate because the listener has good reasons to believe it is genuinely informative (in which case the "drag" might indicate the listener was behaving rationally)?

Unfortunately for our pride in our rationality, the answer is, "No." Several studies have deliberately used random anchors that could not possibly have been perceived to contain useful information. They show that random anchors may change people's opinions as much as credible anchors.

For example, we tried asking people to provide their own anchor. We asked:

"What are the last three digits of your home phone number?"

If the last three digits for a particular person were XYZ, we then said,

"I'm going to add 400 to your answer. Do you think Attila the Hun was defeated in Europe before or after A.D. [XYZ + 400]?"

After they had answered (and without telling them whether they were right), we asked,

"In what year would you guess Attila the Hun was actually defeated?"

The correct answer is A.D. 451. Not surprisingly, few of our MBA candidates knew that.

Surprisingly, however, the telephone-number anchor dramatically affected the years given, as the table below shows. Since the students knew that their own telephone number was used as the starting point, they had no logical reason to pay attention to the anchor. Yet it did influence their judgments.

Range of the Initial Anchor (Last 3 Digits of Phone Number plus 400)	Average Estimate of the Year of Attila's Defeat
400 to 599	629
600 to 799	680
800 to 999	789
1000 to 1199	885
1200 to 1399	988

You can guard against the dangers of anchoring in several ways. Most fundamentally, you can make people aware of the dangers. That can be especially helpful if you see a consistent bias in the estimates your organization produces, and you can warn your people to watch out for it in the future. (If, for example, your forecasts are always too close to the previous year's numbers, tell the people who make them—and their bosses—that they need to guard against this bias.)

In addition, analysts can try multiple anchors. Think of a few plausible numbers you could anchor your estimate on: last year's sales, a continuation of the five-year moving average for sales, a consensus of independent analysts' expectations of sales, an optimistic forecast, a pessimistic forecast, etc.

Qualitative Anchors

Anchoring can affect complex qualitative judgments as well as numerical estimates. Indeed, some researchers have argued that few organizations ever formulate policies by comprehensively analyzing their situation. Most, they say, limit themselves to a choice among alternatives that differ only slightly ("incrementally") from existing policies. A company experiencing turnover of employees, for instance, will try minor rules changes to deal with employee dissatisfaction rather than attempt to determine and fix the real cause.

Because no manager can thoroughly analyze every problem, the incremental approach may be a sound way to make many decisions. But incrementalist anchors can destroy good ideas. When a competitor surprises your firm by introducing a new product, don't anchor your thoughts exclusively on the exact product your competitor has introduced. By the time your "me-too" product comes out, its design may already be outdated. Instead, focus your thoughts on the customer's real needs—find out what the customer wants done and find a better way to do it.

Conclusions: Why Excellent Intelligence-Gathering Is Difficult

Our judgments, estimates, and information often suffer from systematic biases.

We are overconfident: We think we know more than we do. That often means we examine too little information, ask the wrong questions, and fail to think critically in making judgments.

We rely on the most available information rather than the most valuable, especially when information is available because it was acquired recently or in a particularly vivid experience.

We anchor our estimates of what is unknown on something we already know, and usually fail to adjust sufficiently for other factors.

Thus, to master intelligence-gathering we must start by asking three critical questions:

1. How much do we *really* know?

2. Is our *knowledge base* truly *representative*?

3. Are our estimates and judgments sound, or *have we relied excessively on an easily available anchor*?

92

Most of all, mastering the intelligence-gathering phase of decision-making requires a systematic approach and awareness of how overconfidence, anchoring, and availability can bias us. In the next chapter, we will introduce some more sophisticated ways to deal systematically with these problems.

Chapter 5
Improving Your Intelligence-Gathering

It's not what we don't know that gives us trouble, it's what we know that ain't so.

WILL ROGERS

How can you obtain really good intelligence when you and your staff, like all humans, suffer from serious biases in your thinking?

Mere awareness of the problem helps. An educated manager should seek to avoid overconfidence about judgments, limit availability biases by gathering information systematically, and minimize the drag of anchoring.

But the tendency to these errors so pervades human thinking that you may need more than mere awareness to overcome them. This chapter introduces five fairly simple methods that can help transform your intelligence-gathering from hit-or-miss into a reliable part of an excellent decision-making process.

Decision Trap Number 5:

Shortsighted Shortcuts—Relying inappropriately on "rules of thumb" such as implicitly trusting the most readily available information or anchoring too much on convenient facts.

Step One: Require Every Estimate to Include a "Level of Confidence"

The first step in making intelligence-gathering really systematic is to ask: "What does an estimate mean?" Until you know exactly what estimates mean, you can do little to improve them.

Suppose your sales manager announces that he is "reasonably sure" he can sell 200,000 Whatzits next year. You know that doesn't mean he will sell *exactly* 200,000. Should the manufacturing department plan its production for *exactly* 200,000? Of course not. Then what does his estimate tell you? Indeed, does the sales manager himself know exactly what he means?

To create really useful estimates, you need to put them in a form whose meaning can be clearly understood—a form that allows you to evaluate whether a forecaster's record is good or bad. The best way is to state a range and a level of confidence: "I estimate we will sell between 180,000 and 220,000 Whatzits next year. I am 80 percent sure." This kind of estimate can be far more useful than a numerically exact (but not exactly correct) prediction. It allows your organization to plan the future with as much knowledge as currently exists or invest in getting better information in case the uncertainty is too great. And it enables the forecaster to learn much more easily from experience.

The sales manager who forecasts a range and a confidence level is betting his reputation in a way that he is not when he simply says he is "reasonably sure" he will sell 200,000 Whatzits. Suppose that for three years in a row he says he is reasonably sure he will sell 200,000. In reality, sales are 175,000 the first year, 140,000 the second, and 230,000 the third. If he had just given a single-point forecast, your staff could argue endlessly over whether his mistakes were reasonable.

But had he forecast a range of 180,000 to 220,000 each year with a confidence level of 80 percent, you can be pretty sure that something is wrong: Since three years in a row sales failed to fall in the range that was forecast, the sales manager should feel embarrassed. If you are his boss, you'll know that either he needs training in better forecasting or the company should focus on shorter-term forecasts, which should be easier for him.

Of course, erroneous forecasts not only hurt your sales manager's reputation, they may hurt your company as a whole. To protect his reputation, your sales manager will probably learn to forecast confidence ranges more accurately. After a while, you may find that when he says he is "80 percent sure" of something, there's really an 80 percent chance it will happen. Ideally, the sales manager will produce his estimates using the linear model approach we'll discuss in Chapter 6.

Now the sales manager's estimates will enable the manufacturing department to deal realistically with suppliers and the finance department to project realistic cash flows. Without confidence-range estimates, however, good risk assessments are not really possible.

Fine-Tuning Confidence Judgments

Sometimes you need not state a prediction in terms of a range. If, for example, you are recommending the selection of a contractor and you just want to indicate that you are confident the person will show up on a particular day, you may simply say you are 95 percent sure that the firm will show up and do an acceptable job.

But even in this kind of case, providing a confidence level

helps make judgments useful. Both the people making the forecast and the person relying on it know that forecasters can't say they're 95 percent sure ten times and be wrong eight of the ten without facing consequences.

And providing levels of confidence will help you analyze whether you need to seek *additional* information before making a decision on a complex issue. When a confidence-range estimate has been made you can ask, "What additional information would allow us to predict a narrower range with an even higher level of confidence?" Narrower ranges and higher levels of confidence mean less uncertainty for your business. Thus, you will be better able to assess whether the additional information and delay are worth the added costs.

Watch out in employing this tactic with analysts who are not used to it: The analysts may *feel* more confident with more information even if the additional information does not make them any more *accurate* at all. (We'll discuss this point in greater detail later in this chapter.) But as people get used to using confidence-range forecasts, they are more likely to be able to tell you accurately what would help them forecast better—or to say honestly that they can't be certain.

Step Two: Provide Feedback and Training to Help People Calibrate

Once you've introduced ranges and confidence levels in estimates, you need to ensure that the people who make estimates receive timely feedback on their accuracy, that they are trained to improve, and that they are accountable for excellence.

Royal Dutch/Shell, for instance, has saved many millions of dollars by improving the accuracy of oil-drilling decisions through training in prediction skills. After Shell began requiring that geologists state their levels of confidence in their predictions, it discovered (not surprisingly) that newly hired geologists were wrong much more often than their stated levels of confidence predicted. When young geologists said there was a 50 percent chance of finding oil, oil would be found as little as 30 percent of the time. Thus, Shell was spending billions of dollars on dry holes.

The young geologists possessed impeccable credentials. But their primary knowledge vastly exceeded their secondary knowledge—they overestimated what they knew. As they matured and saw which wells actually came in, geologists learned to "calibrate" their predictions. By the time geologists had many years of experience, Shell could trust that if they said wells on a dozen sites each had a 50 percent chance of producing oil, about half of the wells would produce. But "on the job training" was causing far more dry holes than accurately calibrated predictions would have yielded.

So Shell established a new kind of training program. Inexperienced geologists were shown summaries of past cases reflecting the myriad factors that might predict oil deposits. For each, they had to make a prediction with a numerical level of confidence. Then, they received feedback—they were told whether or not oil was actually found at each of the sites.

The training worked wonderfully. Now, when even junior Shell geologists predict there is a 50 percent chance of producing oil at a site, the company gets a hit about five times out of ten.

Training Weather Forecasters and Bankers

When people observe many similar past events, they often learn to estimate accurately the likelihood of future events of that kind.

Believe it or not, such regular feedback (plus training) has given weather forecasters an enviable record of reliability.

When weather forecasters make a forecast, within hours they see the actual outcome. Thus they learn to make good forecasts. If an experienced weather person says there is a 60 percent chance of rain, rain falls 59 percent of the time. When a 90 percent chance of showers is predicted, it rains 87 percent of the time. By requiring levels of confidence in weather prediction, supervisors in the National Weather Service have made the feedback more meaningful and created enormous benefits for themselves, for weather forecasters who wanted to improve, and for users of weather forecasts.

Studying the past can help bankers as well. George Moore, a former chairman of Citicorp, used to keep a list of his bank's ten biggest mistakes—loans that had cost it many millions. All credit officers were required to study the list. After he retired, however, the bank stopped using it. In his book, *The Banker's Life*, Moore commented: "If the officers responsible for Mexico and Brazil and Argentina . . . had known some of the past mistakes . . . they wouldn't have made the loans they made."

Most Professionals Can Learn to Calibrate Better

Professionals learn to calibrate when they receive timely, accurate feedback on their estimates. Groups that typically calibrate well include expert bridge players and experienced accountants.

In most professions, however, you won't get good feedback automatically. Thus you won't learn to calibrate unless you or your organization works to *create* feedback. We'll discuss systems for making sure you learn from the results of your decisions in Chapter 9. But you can obtain an important kind of feedback on your calibration in your own professional field without waiting for the outcome of the decisions you're making today.

Here's one useful approach: Create a test that asks for range estimates and levels of confidence in response to questions relevant to your profession. Give this test to all professionals in your department and to all new employees.

A test for personnel managers might include such questions as:

1. Among professionals hired in the last five years, how many have failed to be promoted on schedule?

2. How many applicants for systems analyst positions did advertisements in major out-of-town newspapers generate?

3. Minorities and women comprise what percentage of our job applicants?

and so on.

Remember that *learning to recognize how much you know and don't know* is the key issue, not actually coming close to the right answers. If your personnel department recognizes that it doesn't know what share of professionals progress on schedule, it can do research to find out. But if personnel managers believe they know and they're wrong, they are likely to adopt incorrect policies without any research at all.

Simply give your best range estimates together with levels of confidence. Then secure the exact answers from appropriate sources. Docs the frequency with which real answers fall within the ranges you provided correspond with the levels of confidence you gave? If the real answers fall within your ranges significantly *less* often than you anticipated, you fail the test.

Remaking a Loan Department

The results of these tests often astound people. (Your own score may be a shocker too.) But these tests can help transform decision-making in organizations.

One bank loan officer who heard us talk about overconfidence applied these principles. His bank's loan portfolio had been declining, but most of his colleagues were certain they knew their market. Their boss was sure his officers had no problems with overconfidence. His comment? "No one is more realistic than a banker."

To indulge his subordinate, however, the boss agreed to an overconfidence test. The boss and every single loan officer flunked. The test showed that every one of them misunderstood the lending limits and other crucial facts about their competitors.

The boss was shaken. He took immediate action. He required each loan officer to contribute information each week to what he labeled a "competitor alert file." He told each officer to check the file weekly until the department understood the competition more realistically.

Within a few weeks a memo inserted in the competitor alert file by a loan officer in a branch office showed that a major customer was considering a switch to a different bank. The other bank was not even one of the major area banks the boss had considered to be competitors. In fact, it was so small it couldn't legally meet the needs of the customer who was considering switching. But the smaller bank had formed a consortium with another small institution to seek the business legally.

Because the loan officer in charge of the account had been alerted, he managed to successfully head off the client's move. He saved about $160,000 in annual revenue. Good feedback on the accuracy of judgments can improve many business endeavors enormously. Yet most of us function in jobs with poor feedback on the quality of our own judgments and decisions.

Step Three: Ask Disconfirming Questions

The "confirmation bias" can lead intelligent people amazingly far astray from the truth. Once you've reoriented your estimating processes to provide accurate ranges and confidence levels rather than dangerous single-point predictions, you should next ensure that you regularly ask an appropriate number of **disconfirming questions**.

A penchant for disconfirming thinking can be a manager's best friend. At one small metalworking firm, for instance, an inventory audit had found a discrepancy between the actual amount of raw material at their plant and the amount that records showed should be there. Plant managers guessed that a thief had stolen the metal, since theft had been a problem in the recent past. The managers alerted their security force. They questioned employees. They even spent a weekend at the plant searching for clues and racking their brains for ideas about how the metal could have been stolen. The inventory system indicated that the amount of metal missing was the equivalent of a year's profits, and they were terrified of reporting it to their boss. But no thief could be found.

On Monday they dejectedly told the company's president of their problem. He asked only one question—but a disconfirming question: "How much raw material would have to have been stolen to account for the discrepancy?"

The question surprised the managers. They hadn't calculated the amount because it seemed irrelevant to the question of who the thief might be. After a few minutes of figuring, they replied, "A small mountain." The inventory system was reporting an impossible volume of metal missing.

The managers had worked so hard pursuing their theft theory that they had not asked basic questions that might test

103

their premise: How much metal was "gone"? Would other explanations of the discrepancy make more sense than thievery? In a single stroke the president's question eliminated the possibility of theft: No one could have moved that many tons of metal off-site undetected. Within hours, they discovered that during a change in accountants, a procedure to update inventory records had been incorrectly applied, causing a huge accounting error.

We believe the president's ability to ask the right question was not just luck. He understood the art of disconfirming questions—questions seeking information that will show our initial judgment is wrong. Especially when numerous possibilities exist, it is a crucial skill to eliminate efficiently the many blind alleys one might get stuck in.

Most of us should work to develop that art. We need to judiciously seek a balance between evidence that will confirm and sharpen our theories, on the one hand, and looking for evidence that may disconfirm them on the other. In any intelligence-gathering process, we need to make a deliberate effort to ask disconfirming questions. Write down some potentially disconfirming questions to ask in each major information-gathering effort you undertake.

A few disconfirming questions might have changed the course of World War II. The entire German military machine failed to ask them after it discovered that Britain was learning the locations of its submarines in the early days of the war. The high command theorized (plausibly) that Britain obtained its intelligence from an extraordinary spy network. And a security campaign did uncover an alarming number of spies.

But the real reason for British success was that British logicians under Alan Turing had cracked Germany's codes. A simple disconfirming question ("Could they have broken our codes?") and an easily conducted test (a false report leaked to the British only in code, for example) might have shown the

Germans some really useful ways to interfere with British intelligence.

What Is Misleading You?

You should ask disconfirming questions not only about your ideas but also about your data sources. Often, estimates and forecasts are biased because a source of data is consistently providing wrong information.

For example, if you rely in hiring computer programmers on data provided by candidates themselves, you are likely to wind up with programmers who are better in self-promotion than in programming. The solution is to establish a policy of checking external data such as references and previous employers.

Often experiments designed to disconfirm your ideas are excellent investments. David Ogilvy, in his memoirs, says he succeeded in advertising because he was always ready to run a few ads he deemed to be losers. Invariably, some were big hits, leading him to revise his theories.

Step Four: **Expose the Hidden Sources of Future Problems**

Good managers try to "expect the unexpected." Of course the unexpected is difficult to anticipate—even though we know it is inevitable!

Thus, too many organizations fail to complete their projects within the time they originally forecast. Too many can't deliver products at the costs they originally hoped. And many get blindsided by nasty surprises and expensive errors.

Availability biases cause people to underestimate the difficulties they will face: Few of the unexpected events that *might* delay a project come easily to mind when people are planning it. And no matter how knowledgeable people may be, they retain the human tendency to underestimate the importance of information that is not readily available to them.

Successful professionals have discovered that a few standard techniques outlined below—the use of fault trees, scenarios, and prospective hindsight—can improve estimates dramatically. These techniques simply make people see the possible causes of problems more clearly.

Good planning techniques consume time in decision-making processes that are conducted under severe time pressure. Thus people are constantly tempted to omit them to "save time." But omitting them often causes unhappiness and losses. For example, in the mid-1960s Boeing engineers made projections of manufacturing costs for the 747 jumbo jet that were too low by nearly 50 percent. Thus the jet was priced far too low, and even after ten years Boeing still had not recovered its investment in this "winner."

In recent years companies such as Hewlett-Packard and Xerox have required efforts to anticipate problems in the early stages of their design processes, because they recognize that the alternative is frustration and high costs.

Fault Trees Reveal Obstacles

One of the simplest ways to make possible problems more available is to construct a fault tree, a diagram that details the many ways in which a complex system might fail. For example, if you wanted to examine the reasons why a restaurant might fail (so you could realistically assess and minimize the risk of investing in a new restaurant), you might construct a fault tree with the primary set of branches representing the major kinds of failures. Then you would list subgroups of causes within each major branch. In each subgroup, include an "all other" category. See the sample on page 109.

Fault trees help people see the possible causes of problems more clearly in their minds and therefore help them to consider realistically the likelihood of difficulties. To maximize a fault tree's usefulness, however, you must list problem areas on the tree as completely as possible. Otherwise, estimates will still suffer from an availability bias.

For example, one of us asked a group of eighty restaurant and hotel managers studying at the Cornell School of Hotel Administration to use a fault tree to estimate the likelihood of a number of causes of restaurant failures, including an "all other" category.

Within a main branch of the fault tree labeled "Decreasing Number of Customers," for instance, one group saw a list of six causes plus "all other." The listed causes included "incorrect pricing," "unclear image," "outdated restaurant concept," etc. The group was specifically warned to "remember to include the likelihood of any reason not specifically listed in the 'all other' category." But the managers listed an average of only 7 percent under "all other."

A second group saw a list of twelve causes under "Decreasing Number of Customers"—the original six plus six additional such as "poor quality of food," "poor quality of service," "changing competition," etc. The longer list of causes made the additional six causes much more available, and these managers assigned them a combined probability of 50 percent. The "all other" category decreased only to 4 percent. So the total probabilities assigned by the first group to its "all other" category should have been on the order of 54 percent. In other words, the first group vastly underestimated such causes of customer decline as poor food and poor service simply because they had not been listed on the original chart we had given them.

However, our research also showed that you can expect to reduce such availability biases dramatically by creating a fuller fault tree. We asked a third group of restaurant managers to estimate likelihoods on a fault tree that listed the original six causes and allowed space for the manager to list up to six more. Some managers who used this chart failed to list any additional causes. They estimated probabilities similar to those of the first, highly biased, group. But those managers who did write in six additional causes of their own choosing—which were often different from those we had listed for the second group—provided probabilities similar to those of the second group. We don't know for sure whether the probabilities produced by any of the managers were accurate. But we do know that thinking about a list of twelve causes would greatly benefit a manager trying realistically to avoid future problems.

Fault trees especially produce useful estimates if you break a large project into parts and try to estimate the time required for each component. You'll usually find that you can estimate some parts of the project accurately because you have done similar work before. You won't need a fault tree for these components. But after you have estimated the components based on your past experience, you can then create fault trees to gauge the problems you'll face in the parts of the project you know less well.

Using Scenarios

Your goal is not just to list systematically what could go wrong, but also to examine the *joint* effect of possible problems. This way you can understand the risks that lie ahead and possibly deal with likely problems early in the process when the costs of avoiding them are low.

Creating optimistic and pessimistic scenarios will help you explore possible interactions among causes and help you think about outcome patterns too complex for a fault tree to handle.

108

FAULT TREE FOR RESTAURANT

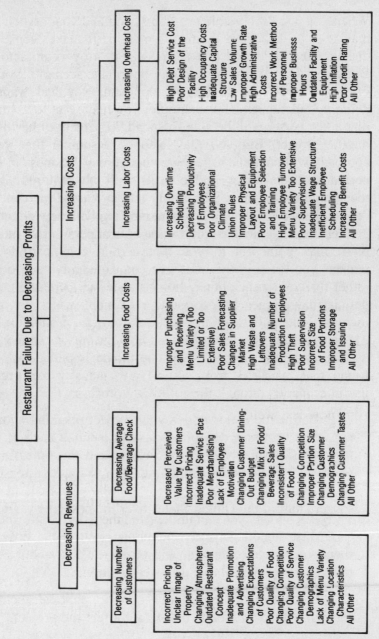

Restaurant Failure Due to Decreasing Profits

Decreasing Revenues

Decreasing Number of Customers

Incorrect Pricing
Unclear Image of Property
Changing Atmosphere
Outdated Restaurant Concept
Inadequate Promotion and Advertising
Changing Expectations of Customers
Poor Quality of Food
Changing Competition
Poor Quality of Service
Changing Customer Demographics
Lack of Menu Variety
Changing Location Characteristics
All Other

Decreasing Average Food/Beverage Check

Decreased Perceived Value by Customers
Incorrect Pricing
Inadequate Service Pace
Poor Merchandising
Lack of Employee Motivation
Changing Customer Dining-Out Budget
Changing Mix of Food/Beverage Sales
Inconsistent Quality of Food
Changing Competition
Improper Portion Size
Changing Customer Demographics
Changing Customer Tastes
All Other

Increasing Costs

Increasing Food Costs

Improper Purchasing and Receiving
Menu Variety Too Limited or Too Extensive)
Poor Sales Forecasting
Changes in Supplier Market
High Waste and Leftovers
Inadequate Number of Production Employees
High Theft
Poor Supervision
Incorrect Size of Food Portions
Improper Storage and Issuing
All Other

Increasing Labor Costs

Increasing Overtime Scheduling
Decreasing Productivity of Employees
Poor Organizational Climate
Union Rules
Improper Physical Layout and Equipment
Poor Employee Selection and Training
High Employee Turnover
Menu Variety Too Extensive
Poor Supervision
Inadequate Wage Structure
Inefficient Employee Scheduling
Increasing Benefit Costs
All Other

Increasing Overhead Cost

High Debt Service Cost
Poor Design of the Facility
High Occupancy Costs
Inadequate Capital Structure
Low Sales Volume
Improper Growth Rate
High Administrative Costs
Incorrect Work Method of Personnel
Improper Business Hours
Outdated Facility and Equipment
High Inflation
Poor Credit Rating
All Other

When you just *list* possible problems, you and your associates may tend to disbelieve them in isolation. It makes sense to discount the likelihood that a fire will destroy your factory. But when you try to draw even an optimistic scenario, you'll often recognize that all the developments you had wanted *could not* all happen. (For example, you may want to assume that a key person will be able to spend 90 percent of her time on the project. But you may also be assuming that your company will continue to receive enough new business in the period that no major budget cuts will be required, and receiving new business may imply that at least 40 percent of the key person's time will be spent meeting with new clients.)

Scenarios that include modest amounts of pessimism, moreover, may point out to you that certain combinations of reasons you listed in the fault tree could magnify each other rather than offset each other. For instance, an increased trade deficit may trigger an economic recession, which in turn increases unemployment and reduces domestic production.

Scenarios can help us understand how the various strands of a complex tapestry move when one thread is pulled. We've found that managers from almost any industry can create useful scenarios through the following process:

1. Define the major issues your project planning should consider. The issue definitions should mention each of the key variables involved in the project and the time frame over which each issue is important. (For example, one issue in an energy scenario might be, "Natural gas prices in the Eastern half of the United States over the next five years.")

2. List major players (including companies, governments, consumers, unions, and others). Think about each player's role, interests, and power position.

3. List potentially important economic, political, technological, and social trends that might affect the project.

110

4. Specify key uncertainties: Variables you cannot predict but that can impact your business positively or negatively (such as the level of the dollar).

5. Now construct two "forced" scenarios by putting all good outcomes in one and all bad outcomes in the other.

6. Assess the internal consistency and plausibility of these artificial scenarios. (For example, the "bad" scenario may include both the assumption that interest rates will be high and the assumption that the country will be mired in a deflationary recession. That's an unlikely combination.)

7. Rearrange the scenario elements to create at least two relatively consistent, plausible scenarios.

8. Evaluate the behavior of the major players in the scenarios created so far to determine whether the players' actions might change them. (For example, a competitor might undercut sales if you were able to increase prices as freely as your most optimistic scenario assumed.)

9. Distill all the information and insight you've gathered so far into a few (anywhere from two to four) distinctly different scenarios that cover a broad range and are each internally consistent.

In the notes to this chapter we have listed some sources helpful in scenario construction.

Prospective Hindsight

On the Monday after the football team has lost, everyone can see why the quarterback's pass to the tight end was a bad idea. Hundreds of "Monday-morning quarterbacks" declare that the quarterback should have anticipated the problem (since it's so easy for them to see it now). Whereas hindsight usually obstructs learning (as discussed in chapter 8), it can actually be turned to advantage in contemplating the future.

Experiments suggest that you can harness your ability to explain events so easily in hindsight to better anticipate *possibilities* that lie still ahead. Such prospective hindsight can be a valuable supplement to fault trees and scenarios.

Simply pretend that whatever you are evaluating has already occurred. For example, assume your project turned out to be a fiasco. Now try to list reasons *why* it occurred. You'll probably see *more reasons* for an event when you pretend it has already happened than when you simply ask yourself why it *might* occur. See the box on page 113 for an experiment you can try for yourself.

To test this technique, we used it with several groups of managers and MBA students. We gave each a brief description of a new employee including what kind of job, company, industry and personal ambitions. Using such vignettes, we asked half to generate plausible reasons why the new employee *might quit* six months from now. They generated an average of 3.5 reasons per person. The other half were told that the new employee *had quit* and were asked to generate plausible reasons why this might have occurred. The hindsight group generated 25 percent more reasons on average (a mean of 4.4 reasons). Moreover, the reasons were different in tone: more specific and linked to the episode presented.

We believe that effects due to prospective hindsight will even be stronger with real decisions involving large stakes. So if you doubt whether your people have sufficient insight into the myriad of causes that could produce success or failure for your project, ask them to engage in some "mental time travel."

Step Five: Limit Yourself to the Information You Can Handle

Lastly, ask whether you may be collecting too much information. If you are fully *rational*, more correct information can only help. However, for *normal* people, too much information can actually hurt, as the following study showed.

Paul Slovic and associates (then at the Oregon Research Institute) tested the predictive abilities of eight professional horse-race handicappers, racetrack employees who set the preliminary betting odds for each race. These handicappers must judge the likelihood that each horse will win the race. To do this, they use "past performance charts," which give nearly a hundred pieces of information on each horse and its history.

In the study, eight handicappers made predictions for numerous races. First, they were allowed to use only five

113

pieces of information per horse from the charts—any five they wanted (often different pieces of information for different handicappers). Then they made the same predictions using ten pieces of information per horse. And then again with their most preferred twenty pieces, and one last time using forty pieces of information for each horse in the race.

Did the horse-race handicappers become more accurate in picking winners as they were given more information? They themselves felt that they would be. For each race, they were asked not only to pick the winner but also to estimate the chance that they were right. Their confidence increased as the information available rose.

But in reality, there was *no* significant improvement in their accuracy. Accuracy failed to rise, and their secondary knowledge—their realism about their predictive abilities—actually declined (see widening gap in Fig. 1 below).

We believe the additional information simply *overloaded* the handicapper, causing inconsistency and error. Other researchers have found similar results in other disciplines—for instance, with clinical psychologists who were asked to predict the behavior of patients with brain damage.

More information helps only to the extent that you can use it intelligently. Many professionals ask for too much in making estimates and decisions (to cover themselves or postpone having to make a decision). Numerous studies suggest that people have difficulty keeping more than seven or so "chunks" of information in mind at once. Vast amounts of data may only confuse matters, as the next chapter will demonstrate.

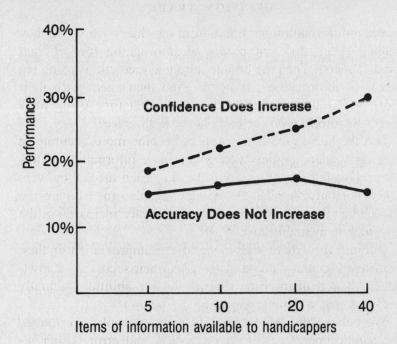

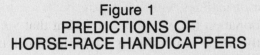

Figure 1
PREDICTIONS OF
HORSE-RACE HANDICAPPERS

Conclusions: How to Gather Intelligence Well

In this chapter, we've shown that a number of intelligence-gathering tactics can improve your success beyond what you can achieve simply by being aware of the dangers of overconfidence, the bias toward confirming evidence, the availability bias, and the anchoring trap.

A good decision-maker should:

—insist that people state estimates in terms of *ranges* and *levels of confidence*, so their meaning can be clear;

—create *feedback, training, and accountability* for people who make these estimates, so they can improve their skills;

—ask questions that might *disconfirm* initial presumptions (in case they are wrong);

—use techniques such as *fault trees, scenario building,* and *prospective hindsight* to seek reasons why projects may be more complex and difficult than you suspect at first;

—avoid collecting extensive amounts of information for estimates and decisions unless you have a way to synthesize it in a coherent fashion.

If you understand well the biases that all of us are prone to, and you take the above steps to counteract them, you'll create truly sound intelligence and lay a foundation for excellent decisions.

Part III

COMING TO CONCLUSIONS

Chapter 6
Making the Choice

Many complain about their memory,
few about their judgment.
LA ROCHEFOUCAULD

Suppose your frame captures the essence of your problem. And you've collected excellent intelligence. Will you make the best choice?

Not always. Too many people pose their questions carefully, collect their intelligence brilliantly, but then "wing it" when it comes to actually deciding. They know no other way. And so they make decisions that don't give them a good chance to achieve their goals.

Most people make decisions intuitively. Intuition is fine for small decisions—where to buy groceries, how to organize your filing cabinet, or whether to send a memo instead of telephoning someone. But over a hundred studies have led to an important conclusion about making choices or predictions: You can develop procedures that will make your decision better than your own unaided intuition. If you follow sound procedures, you'll have a better chance of achieving your goals than if you just make a choice because it "feels right."

When you have to choose among *many options*, a systematic approach created with one of the tools we'll discuss in this chapter is likely to produce significant benefits.

When you make a *unique* decision among *only a few alternatives*, you may need no more than to list the pros and cons of each alternative, take account of the relative signifi-

119

cance of each "pro" and each "con," and choose the alternative with the preponderance of "pros."

All decision-making depends profoundly on good intuition, since no one can frame a problem well or gather intelligence wisely without it. But whenever something substantial rides on a final choice, it's worthwhile to base your decision on some kind of systematic procedure.

What Is "Intuition"?

When you rely on intuition or "gut feel" to make a decision, your mind processes part or all of the information you possess automatically, quickly, and without awareness of any details. But intuitive, seat-of-the-pants decisions seldom take proper account of all the information available. They suffer from inconsistency. (On different days, the same expert will decide differently even a clear-cut question such as whether an X ray indicates the presence of cancer.) Intuitive decisions are affected not only by the evidence that *should* affect your choice, but also by factors such as fatigue, boredom, distractions, and recollection of a fight with your spouse at breakfast.

On the other hand, intuitive decision-making *does* have at least one advantage. It certainly takes less time than making a decision with the systematic methods we'll discuss below. Everyone *must* decide many small questions intuitively. In theory, moreover, an intuitive decision can take account of knowledge you possess but can't put into words. And in principle your mind may be able to process information in a more complex and subtle way than you could formalize in a decision rule.

The Limits of Intuition

The disadvantages of intuitive decision-making, however, are more profound than most people realize. People who make decisions intuitively (doctors making diagnoses, executives hiring subordinates, sales people sizing up prospects, etc.) achieve much less consistency than they generally suspect.

Numerous studies have demonstrated this. One, for example, concerned the consistency of medical diagnoses. Psychologists presented information extracted from ninety-six individual X-ray photographs to five radiologists. In each case, the doctors were asked to evaluate the likelihood that a malignant stomach ulcer was present.

Then a week later (after the radiologists had a chance to forget the details of the cases), the doctors were presented with the same ninety-six cases in a different order—as if they were new. Again the psychologists asked them to judge the likelihood of malignancy.

The psychologists then compared the conclusions the radiologists had reached on the same cases on different days. The results were tabulated along a scale between 0 to 1, with 1 indicating perfect correlation and 0 meaning no correlation at all.*

The correlations ranged from .60 to .92. When doctors had the opportunity to make the same decision twice, their second judgment would differ from their first a substantial part of the time.

Studies like this suggest that advice to seek a second—or even a third—opinion before undergoing surgery is well

*A correlation coefficient is a standard statistical measure of agreement between one set of numbers and another. It ranges from -1 to 1, with a correlation coefficient of 0 denoting no correlation whatsoever. A correlation coefficient of -1 implies total disagreement— exactly the *opposite* judgment from one week to the next.

121

founded. Doctors and other professionals seldom realize just how much their intuitive judgments can vary from day to day. Since most of the variation goes unrecognized, it is improbable that professionals are doing all they can to guarantee that they make the choices most likely to produce good outcomes.

Indeed, in one early study reported in the *New England Journal of Medicine,* when boys were examined for a possible tonsillectomy, doctors showed no consistency whatsoever in diagnoses: When a panel of physicians examined 389 boys, they judged that 45 percent of them needed a tonsillectomy. When another panel examined *only* the boys judged healthy by the first panel, they actually concluded that 46 percent needed a tonsillectomy. (To be consistent with the first panel, they should have concluded that *none* of the 214 boys needed a tonsillectomy.)

Finally a third panel examined only the 116 boys who had been judged healthy by the first two groups. It found that 44 percent needed a tonsillectomy.

For many decisions, professionals show more consistency than the doctors in the tonsillectomy experiment. But nearly every study shows inconsistencies far higher than professionals themselves imagine. People making decisions by intuition alone usually suffer from "information overload" and have a hard time applying simple rules consistently even when they try.

Decision Trap Number 6:

Shooting From the Hip—Believing you can keep straight in your head all the information you've discovered, and therefore "winging it" rather than following a systematic procedure when making the final choice.

Some Simple—but Limited—Alternatives to Intuition

In addition to intuition, people use other simple approaches to making choices. The two most important are:

—simple screening and ranking rules, and

—occupation-specific rules of thumb.

Like pure intuition, both have their place. They are particularly useful to make quick decisions among large numbers of choices. But they cannot guarantee excellence by themselves.

Suppose you want to decide where to eat in a strange city. A simple screening rule is: First eliminate all restaurants that are either very cheap or very expensive, next eliminate all restaurants that do not serve fresh fish, next eliminate those that require more than twenty minutes driving time, etc. You'll quickly narrow your choices to one or two.

Unfortunately, this kind of approach is *insensitive*. For instance, you may miss a great restaurant twenty-five minutes away, or one just above your budget limit. Still, many financial institutions use this kind of rule to evaluate applicants

123

for personal loans. They screen each applicant with respect to certain preselected criteria and approve a loan only if the person meets *all* of the minimum requirements. For example, a bank may stipulate that a loan will be granted only if the applicant:

1. has no previous payment defaults *and*
2. has at least 25 percent of income uncommitted *and*
3. has lived at least one year at his or her present address *and*
4. has worked at least one year at his or her present job *and*
5. is a skilled laborer or white-collar worker.

This kind of screening test is called a "threshold rule."

Threshold rules can be useful, especially in quickly eliminating numerous unsuitable alternatives. But it's easy for organizations to overlook their serious weaknesses. Consider, for example, the following two loan applicants:

Ms. Smith	Ms. Jones
no defaults; several ninety-day delinquent-payment warnings	no defaults; no delinquent warnings
25 percent uncommitted income	70 percent uncommitted income
one year at present address	20 years at present address
one year at current job	15 years at current job
skilled laborer	unskilled laborer

Note that Ms. Smith meets all requirements but only marginally. Ms. Jones, in contrast, meets and exceeds all criteria except for the job classification, and therefore will be denied a loan.

This example illustrates the rigidity inherent in most simple screening and ranking rules; surpluses in one category do not compensate or offset deficiencies in other areas; hence, superior candidates may be rejected while consistently mediocre candidates pass. When applied to personnel decisions or school admissions, threshold rules have the further disadvantage that they result in unnecessarily homogeneous groups (i.e., all members meet a narrow set of requirements even though some diversity among employees or students is probably desirable).

Threshold rules and other screening systems eliminate the random inconsistency of purely intuitive approaches. But because they do not make use of all available information and are "noncompensatory" (many excellent ratings on some attributes cannot compensate for one poor rating), screening rules are appropriate only for rough sorting or ranking tasks.

Sometimes these non-compensatory rules may appear sophisticated. If ranking rules are not closely examined, they can lead to disaster. One multibillion-dollar food products company, for instance, lost market share in five unrelated product categories. The problem was largely due to a decision rule used to determine whether to introduce new versions of products that were cheaper to produce. The rule was:

Replace the current product with the cost-reduced version if and only if consumers [in careful test-marketing] rate the cost-reduced version to be approximately as good as the current product in taste quality.

Consumers really found Old-Fashioned Version A and Cost-Reduced Version B to be quite similar. But then the next group of brand managers (generally young people who seldom remained in their jobs more than twenty-four months) would replace Version B with Further Cost-Reduced Version C. Consumers found Version B and Version C to be similar as well. But they *might* be able to tell the difference between Version A and Version C. By the time a new group of brand managers introduced Super-Cost-Reduced Version D a few years later, consumers could definitely tell that quality wasn't what it used to be. And since some competitors still sold products equal in quality to Version A, consumers switched.

Occupation-Specific Rules of Thumb

Some simple decision rules deserve an honored place in decision-making. Every industry or profession has rules of thumb that guide people when problems are too complex for a truly "analytical" solution in the time available. These rules offer some of the best decision guidance available anywhere.

But people misuse them. They often trust the rules of thumb as if they were certainties, and fail to recognize when they should make an independent analytical decision.

Many professionals develop a powerful repertoire of rules of thumb which often lead to better decisions than unaided intuition. For example, commercial real estate people teach that "the corner lot is worth the sum of the two contiguous lots" because of its greater visibility. Procter & Gamble has established a rule of thumb that says: "When introducing a new food product, require that consumers prefer its taste 2 to 1 over the chief competitor."

Many industries use rules of thumb in pricing. Restaurants, for instance, often price meals by taking the cost of the raw food and multiplying by three. Ideally, of course, prices should be set to maximize profits over the long term. But that, though simple in theory, is enormously complex in practice. So decision shortcuts are widely used. The box on page 127 provides some further examples of business rules of thumb.

If you're deciding how to price your corner lot or your restaurant's meals, you probably should seek a solution consistent with industry rules of thumb unless you find strong evidence in favor of another alternative. The rules may

126

BUSINESS RULES OF THUMB

When writing an ad, use sentences of no more than twelve words.

DAVID OGILVY
Founder, Ogilvy & Mather International

The individual with responsibility for implementing a decision should be a part of the decision-making process.

EUGENE WEBB
Associate Dean, Stanford Business School

Give a name to all major company projects. It gives everyone an easy way to refer to a common set of goals.

BOARDROOM REPORTS

Never make a personnel judgment the first time it comes up. Never fire someone without sleeping on it.

ALFRED P. SLOAN, JR.
Former Chairman of the Board, General Motors

To maximize the size of your next job's salary:
  1. Let them make the first bid.
  2. Ask for 20 percent more than they offer.

PAUL HELLMAN

Put your home on the market in the spring: 71 percent of all home sales occur between April and July.

KAY WILLIAMS

Set a maximum of three to five corporate goals in a year.

JOHN HANLEY
Former President, Monsanto

Round numbers beg to be negotiated, usually by counteroffer round numbers. Odd numbers sound harder, firmer, less negotiable.

MARK MCCORMACK

Build a 20 percent pessimism quotient into all expectations. Overestimate by 20 percent the amount of time it will take to accomplish a plan. Underestimate by 20 percent the expected results.

ROBERT TOWNSEND
Former President, Avis Rent-a-Car
Author, Up the Organization

embody wisdom you can't fully absorb into your decision process in any other way.

But too many professionals mechanically employ rules of thumb when they should make a more careful, independent judgment. Others fail to understand enough about *why* a rule works to predict when it will fail.

The real estate developer Trammell Crow became a success largely by violating at least one rule of thumb in a niche where he saw that it didn't make sense. A time-honored commercial real estate rule of thumb said: "Don't build a building without a tenant." Crow realized, however, that many Texas companies had a voracious demand for warehouse space but would be reluctant to lease warehouses before they were built. He built warehouses on speculation and made a fortune.

Never consider a rule of thumb sacred. (Even Trammell Crow's rules could be overrated, as his partners discovered when he went into semiretirement and they pushed his firm into near-bankruptcy in the real estate boom and bust of the 1980s.)

Rules of thumb are truly valuable. But in any genuinely new situation, the decision procedures we'll discuss below succeed far better than blind pursuit of simple rules of thumb. As the ad man David Ogilvy put it,

> Rules are for the obedience of fools and the guidance of wise men.

"Linear Models": Reliable Approaches to Making a Choice

Benjamin Franklin proposed an approach to decision-making that has stood up well under close analysis. The box on page 129 contains a letter he wrote in 1772 to the British chemist

London, September 19, 1772

Dear Sir,

In the affair of so much importance to you, wherein you ask my advice, I cannot, for want of sufficient premises, advise you what to determine, but if you please I will tell you how. When those difficult cases occur, they are difficult, chiefly because while we have them under consideration, all the reasons pro and con are not present to the mind at the same time; but sometimes one set present themselves, and at other times another, the first being out of sight. Hence the various purposes or inclinations that alternatively prevail, and the uncertainty that perplexes us.

To get over this, my way is to divide half a sheet of paper by a line into two columns; writing over the one Pro, and over the other Con. Then, during the three or four days consideration, I put down under the different heads short hints of the different motives, that at different times occur to me, for or against the measure. When I have thus got them all together in one view, I endeavor to estimate their respective weights; and where I find two, one on each side, that seem equal, I strike them both out. If I find a reason pro equal to some two reasons con, I strike out the three. If I judge some two reasons con, equal to some three reasons pro, I strike out the five; and thus proceeding I find at length where the balance lies; and if, after a day or two of further consideration, nothing new that is of importance occurs on either side, I come to a determination accordingly.

And, though the weight of reasons cannot be taken with the precision of algebraic quantities, yet when each is thus considered, separately and comparatively, and the whole lies before me, I think I can judge better, and am less liable to make a rash step, and in fact I have found great advantage from this kind of equation, in what may be called moral or prudential algebra.

Wishing sincerely that you may determine for the best, I am ever, my dear friend, yours affectionately.

B. Franklin

Joseph Priestley suggesting strategies to deal with a complex choice. Franklin recognized the dangers of the purely intuitive approach. He recommended making a list of pros and cons relating to a choice and then crossing out pros and cons of equal weight. He would choose the alternative which still had reasons left after the reasons on the other side of the sheet had been canceled.

We don't know for how many decisions Franklin actually used this method, but it would have been extremely suitable, for example, to his decision whether or not to go to London in 1724 or to acquire an interest in the *Pennsylvania Gazette* in 1729. It would be appropriate today, for instance, for a restaurant manager deciding whether to increase his prices above the level that the traditional rule of thumb suggests. In fact, Franklin's method is a good way to make any decision where only two alternatives exist: Whether to take a new job, whether to attend graduate school, whether to launch a new product, etc.

In making final choices, the biggest problems are overcoming:

—your own random inconsistency and

—your inability to effectively process the large quantity of available information.

Considerable research suggests that you will maximize your chances of making the best choice if you find a systematic way to evaluate all the evidence favorable or unfavorable to each possible choice, compare the strength of evidence on each side rigorously, then pick the choice that your system indicates the evidence favors.

Decision theorists call this kind of choice system a subjective linear model. It is *subjective* because the importance assigned to each pro and each con come from a human being's head, not from direct calculations based on the real world. *Linear* is simply a mathematical term for combining the separate pieces of evidence through addition and subtraction— the importance weights of "pros" are added together and the weights of "cons" are subtracted.

Subjective Linear Models

Franklin's method works well for a simple "yes or no" decision. For decisions involving more than two choices, an equivalent procedure is to:

1. List each factor that provides evidence for or against various alternatives.

2. Assign weights to each factor to reflect their relative importance.

3. Make a numerical rating of the extent to which the evidence about each factor favors (or argues against) each alternative.

4. Multiply the score each alternative receives on each factor by the weight assigned to that factor, then add up all the results to get an overall score for each alternative.

Here's an example: We created subjective linear models to forecast the academic performance of applicants to our MBA program. These models mirror those of college admissions officers who must decide whom to admit.

For each applicant, we created files similar to admissions files with the names disguised. A summary of the contents of the files appears in Table 1(a). (In reality, each file was from an applicant who was eventually admitted to the program and who enrolled as a student. Thus we could test the performance of our predictions against actual results.)

A subjective linear model for this purpose is really an index designed to predict the performance of various candidates for

Table 1
A SUBJECTIVE LINEAR MODEL

(a) Summary Sheet of Applicant Information

Applicant	Personal Essay	Selectivity of Undergraduate Institution	Undergraduate major	College Grade Average	Work Experience	GMAT Verbal	GMAT Quant.
1	Poor	Highest	Science	2.50	10	98%	60%
2	Excellent	Above Average	Business	3.82	0	70%	80%
3	Average	Below Average	Other	2.96	15	90%	80%
.	.	.	.	.	.	.	.
.	.	.	.	.	.	.	.
.	.	.	.	.	.	.	.
117	Weak	Least	Business	3.10	100	98%	99%
118	Strong	Above Average	Other	3.44	60	68%	67%
119	Excellent	Highest	Science	2.16	5	85%	25%
120	Strong	Not very	Business	3.96	12	30%	58%

(b) Rescaled Table for Subjective Linear Model

Applicant	Essay	Selectivity	Major	Grade Point	Work Experience	GMAT Verbal	GMAT Quant.	Overall* Score
1	0	100	100	25	10	98	60	59.1
2	100	60	50	91	0	70	80	67.8
3	50	40	0	48	15	90	80	49.0
·	·	·	·	·	·	·	·	·
·	·	·	·	·	·	·	·	·
117	25	0	50	55	100	98	99	59.7
118	75	60	0	72	60	68	67	60.0
119	100	100	100	8	5	85	25	51.0
120	75	20	50	98	12	30	58	54.0
Weights Used	5%	20%	10%	25%	10%	10%	20%	

*The overall score was obtained by multiplying the weights shown in the last row with each attribute score, and summing these product terms across attributes to arrive at a weighted average.

admission to the school. To create an index that will predict grade-point averages, each item of information must be converted to a scale where 0 represents the lowest score and 100 represents the highest. This is simple for numeric information such as college grade average, and Graduate Management Admission Test (GMAT) scores. Essays, work experience, undergraduate majors, and the selectivity of undergraduate institutions must first be graded subjectively. Then they too can be scaled. Those least favorable to achieving a high grade-point average in graduate school will be given zero and those most favorable to a high grade-point average will be given 100. The results of this indexing process appear in Table 1(b).

Now we just have to apply weights to each column to indicate which factors we believe are the most important. One sample set of weights appears in the bottom row. Using those sample weights, we produce an overall score (multiplying each number by the corresponding weight and then adding) that appears in the last column. Based on this weighting, Applicant Number 2 would be most preferred of those listed, Applicant Number 118 would be next, etc.

This procedure keeps track of all the information for you and allows a computer to crunch the numbers, freeing your attention for the critical judgment: picking the factors you consider significant enough to include in the model and deciding what weights to assign them. Note that a subjective linear model like this can also be used for making estimates such as those we discussed in the intelligence-gathering chapters. As we'll see, subjective linear models tend to outperform intuition for both forecasting and decision-making.

Bootstrapping

Much research indicates that a subjective linear model will work well as long as you make sure to include all important

134

factors. To create a model quickly, you can assign the weights intuitively as we did in Table 1(b).

But a more reliable way to choose the weights for a subjective linear model is through a procedure called bootstrapping. It's especially useful when experts are good at making judgments but they can't articulate why they make them. Instead of directly assigning weights, we can allow the experts to make careful judgments on a series of cases, then *infer statistically* through a "regression analysis" what weights they were implicitly using to arrive at the particular ranking. The regression analysis will show how much weight, on average, the experts put on each of the underlying factors. (Anyone who has studied statistics in a business school or elsewhere can conduct a regression analysis. Standard computer software packages exist for this.)

In bootstrapping, you seek to build a model of an expert using his or her own intuitive predictions, and then to use that model to *outperform* the expert on new cases.

This sounds magical—you're pulling yourself to a higher level of performance by your own bootstraps. But it works because of one simple idea. When a person makes a prediction, you get wisdom mixed in with random noise. Intuitive judgments suffer from serious random inconsistencies due to fatigue, boredom, and all the factors that make us human. The ideal decision process would eliminate the random noise but retain the real insights that underlie the prediction. This is precisely what bootstrapping does: *It eliminates the noise, and retains the core wisdom of the human expert.* Moreover, it produces a standard procedure for judgment. When you put in the same facts a week later, you always get the same judgment. And dozens of studies show that this odd system actually produces excellent judgments.

Many researchers have compared intuitive judgments to those based on linear bootstrapped models. And the subjective linear models produced by bootstrapping have outperformed or equaled the performance of intuitive judgments *in almost every study*. Table 2 summarizes the findings of nine of these studies.

We conducted one of these research projects ourselves using the case of predicting grade-point-averages discussed above. We asked MBA students currently enrolled at the University of Chicago to predict grade-point averages of "applicants." First we asked them to predict intuitively by studying the items in Table 1(a). Then we conducted regression analyses of each student's prediction to determine what share of their predictions, on average, was attributable to each of the items of applicant information.

We then created a new set of predictions using the new "bootstrapped" models of each graduate student. For 81 percent of the 130 students, the bootstrapped model of their own decision process predicted better than they managed to predict intuitively. The model on average raised the "correlation coefficients" by about six points—some 18 percent. Moreover, this is not what the students expected. They believed in their own inner complexity and vast experience with grading systems. Yet they were unable to beat a simple linear model containing nothing but their own implicit weights. In essence, they beat themselves. The models captured their own insights and applied them with deadly consistency.

Table 2 shows that those results are typical of a wide range of studies, including studies conducted on such experts as oncologists (cancer specialists) and Wall Street analysts.

Substituting a simple but consistent model for a human expert's intuition consistently results in improved prediction (and thus better decisions). Doing something systematic is better in almost all cases than seat-of-the-pants prediction.

136

Table 2
BOOTSTRAPPING STUDIES

Types of Judgments Experts Had to Make	Degree of Correlation with the True Outcomes		
	Intuitive Prediction	"Bootstrapped" Model	Objective Model
Academic Performance of Graduate Students	.19	.25	.54
Life-Expectancy of Cancer Patients	−.01	.13	.35
Changes in Stock Prices	.23	.29	.80
Mental Illness using Personality Tests	.28	.31	.46
Grades and Attitudes in Psychology Course	.48	.56	.62
Business Failures using Financial Ratios	.50	.53	.67
Student's Ratings of Teaching Effectiveness	.35	.56	.91
Performance of Life Insurance Salesman	.13	.14	.43
IQ Scores using Rorschach Tests	.47	.51	.54
Mean (across many studies)	.33	.39	.64

Objective Models: Still Better Decisions

Just using a subjective model won't make our decisions perfect, of course. Although decisions based on a subjective linear model can come out far better than intuitive decisions, they're still wrong some of the time. Can you do still better? The answer is usually no. But

—if the same decision is made *repeatedly*,

—if *data on the outcomes of past decisions are available*, and

—if you have good reason to expect that *the future will resemble the past*,

then you can build an **objective linear model** of the choice. Numerous studies have shown that objective linear models perform even better than subjective linear models.

You construct an objective linear model in exactly the same way as a subjective linear model. But instead of inferring the weights from the subjective predictions of an expert (as you would in a bootstrapped subjective linear model), you infer them statistically from actual past results. This is what insurance companies do, for instance, when estimating risk levels on the basis of actuarial data.

Many forecasters nonetheless are cautious in using objective regression analyses like these to predict the future. While a regression analysis may show to what extent something like the choice of undergraduate major *has been associated* in the past with success in graduate school, it may not predict success in the future. For example, the curriculum in graduate school might have changed, causing a different kind of student to succeed. Especially in predicting complex economic phenomena such as prices or market shares, there is considerable evidence that an objective linear model based on the past may be a poor or dangerous predictor.

In literally dozens of other areas, however, objective linear models prove excellent predictors. Just as subjective linear models have outperformed intuition in dozens of tests, objective linear models have outperformed both intuition and subjective models in an equal number of tests. In particular, wherever you are predicting the behavior of human beings— who will succeed in a job, who will buy your product, or whether a patient will respond to a cancer drug—objective linear models work better than any other approach. They predict the future better than either intuition or subjective models. They are the best available guides to such tasks as hiring decisions, medical diagnoses, and the design of direct mail advertising campaigns.

In all the studies listed in Table 2, objective linear models as well as subjective linear models were created. As the correlation coefficients show, the objective models worked much better than the subjective models.

Banks and other corporations use objective models extensively in evaluating credit applications. So does the IRS in developing its systems to choose whom to audit. They work much better than simple screening rules. Table 3 summarizes the scoring system a major U.S. retailer uses. Statisticians analyzed a large database of past credit purchases or loans, and based on information about payment histories and defaults, assign a number of points for each possible answer to the questions on the loan application. If an applicant receives more than a certain number of points, the application is approved.

Their statistical analysis has indicated many factors predict credit problems quite differently from how our intuitions would lead us to suspect. For example, the applicant who gives no bank reference gets more points than the applicant

Table 3
CREDIT SCORING SYSTEM OF MAJOR RETAIL CHAIN

Zip Code

Zip Codes A	60
Zip Codes B	48
Zip Codes C	41
Zip Codes D	37
Not answered	53

Bank Reference

Checking only	0
Savings only	0
Checking and savings	15
Bank name or loan only	0
No bank reference	7
Not answered	7

Type of Housing

Owns / buying	44
Rents	35
All other	41
Not answered	39

Occupation

Clergy	46
Creative	41
Driver	33
Executive	62
Guard	46
Homemaker	50
Labor	33
Manager	46
Military enlisted	46
Military officer	62
Office staff	46
Outside	33
Production	41
Professional	62
Retired	62
Sales	46
Semiprofessional	50
Service	41
Student	46
Teacher	41

Unemployed	33
All other	46
Not answered	47

Time at Present Address

Less than 6 months	39
6 months–1 year 5 months	30
1 year 6 months–3 years 5 months	27
3 years 6 months–7 years 5 months	30
7 years 6 months–12 years 5 months	39
12 years 6 months or longer	50
Not answered	36

Time with Employer

Less than 6 months	31
6 months–5 years 5 months	24
5 years 6 months–8 years 5 months	26
8 years 6 months–15 years 5 months	31
15 years 6 months or longer	39
Homemakers	39
Retired	31
Unemployed	29
Not answered	29

Finance Company Reference

Yes	0
Other references only	25
No	25
Not answered	15

Other Department Store / Oil Card /
Major Credit Card

Department store only	12
Oil card only	12
Major credit card only	17
Department store and oil card	17
Department store and credit card	31
Major credit card and oil card	31
All three	31
Other references only	0
No credit	0
Not answered	12

who lists a checking account only or a savings account only. Note also that teachers like us get only forty-one points in the "Occupation" category, while students get forty-six and "homemakers" get fifty. Although as educators this point allocation is hard to accept, the scientific way in which this table was constructed strongly suggests its prediction will be superior to ours. (When applying for loans, we shall reframe ourselves as "professionals.")

Objective linear models are also ideal for creating all kinds of estimates and forecasts. Indeed, both objective and subjective linear models are excellent tools for preparing the estimates you'll need in the intelligence-gathering phase we discussed in Chapters 4 and 5. A regression analysis will even give you the range and level of confidence we recommended for all estimates and forecasts in Chapter 5. Statistical analysis (of either an objective model or a bootstrapped subjective model) can also demonstrate that some of the items of information you have been collecting *don't* help in making predictions. If so, you can often avoid the cost of collecting those data.

Multiattribute Utility Analysis

Subjective linear models and objective linear models are the best tools for most significant decisions. But for unusually important and unique decisions (deciding on your corporation's long-term strategy, for example), it may be worthwhile to work with a decision consultant to do a multiattribute utility analysis. These analyses break a choice into key parts. The consultants conducting the process pose detailed trade-off questions to determine the organization's real preferences. (How much profit would you be willing to give up next year to obtain a 10 percent increase in market share?) Multiattribute utility analysis can be extremely useful if a decision is unique, complex, and important.

141

Seeking to make vast complexity manageable, however, consultants typically use specific single numbers for all estimates rather than confidence ranges. Therefore, the final report from a multiattribute utility analysis may suggest far greater precision in its understanding of the future than the analysis really justifies. An analysis of twenty-five strategy alternatives will produce an extremely precise-looking ranking of the alternatives from "optimal" to "least optimal."

Decision-makers can normally choose intuitively among any of the top several in the ranking.

Choosing the Right Techniques for Your Decision

Multiattribute utility analysis is necessary for only a tiny share of all decisions, however. We believe that in general, decision-makers should:

1. Make simple decisions, where little is at stake, intuitively or with simple decision rules.

2. Use statistical decision rules based on an objective linear model to make any important decisions or judgments that are faced repeatedly if data exist to create an objective linear model and there is no clear evidence that the factors influencing the phenomenon in the future will differ from those that influenced it in the past. (This would include many routine psychological or medical diagnoses, hiring decisions, etc.)

3. Construct at least a rudimentary subjective linear model when making important decisions that cannot be addressed with an objective linear model (for example, when deciding which city to relocate to or which job to take).

The Future of Decision-Making

Unfortunately, that's not how the key decision-makers in our lives make their decisions. In many fields such as credit rating, magazine-subscription solicitation, and professional stock analysis where organizations have a great deal of money at stake and understand the issues involved, managers have begun relying on formal models to make decisions.

Professionals have turned to formal models far less, however, in situations truly central to people's lives. People eagerly put their faith in experts such as doctors, counselors, lawyers, and financial advisers for some of the most important decisions they may face. None of these groups have been quick to recognize the increased quality of decision-making they could achieve with more formal decision rules and systematic models.

Thus it's likely that the decision to issue you a credit card is made in a more reliable way than the decision to operate on your stomach.

We don't wish to minimize the importance of doctors and other highly trained experts. Indeed, the importance of skilled professionals for framing questions and collecting evidence is constantly increasing. But professionals should rethink their roles: Their intuitive skills are needed in framing questions and collecting intelligence. These skills are crucial in identifying the pertinent factors in a decision.

But, once the proper frame has been chosen and proper intelligence has been collected, the final choice calls principally for discipline in following the right rules. Shooting from the hip, when much data are involved, is simply unprofessional.

143

Chapter 7
Group Decisions

Gentlemen, I take it we are all in complete agreement on the decision here . . . Then I propose we postpone further discussion of this matter until our next meeting to give ourselves time to develop disagreement and perhaps gain some understanding of what the decision is all about.
ALFRED P. SLOAN, JR.

Many people seek a simple solution to the uncertainties of decision-making: They bring more people into the process. With many good minds working together, they think, an excellent decision will surely emerge.

Unfortunately, they're wrong. No matter how brilliant their members may be, groups aren't superhuman. Groups are likely to outperform individuals only to the extent that productive conflict arises among their members and such conflicts get resolved through balanced debate and careful intelligence-gathering. When that happens, a group is likely to understand the issues better than an individual, and more likely to choose wisely. When it doesn't happen, groups are just as likely to err as individuals—and sometimes more so.

Successful group deliberation depends on the skillful management of conflict and dissent. In early stages, group members' ideas should be encouraged to diverge. Then only as facts, estimates, and well-considered arguments become available should the group move toward a conclusion. If the group as a whole is satisfied that the decision was made through a fair, thoughtful process, it's likely the decision itself will be effective.

Why Groups Fail

Frequently groups of smart, well-motivated people are mismanaged. Members agree prematurely on the wrong solution. Then they give each other feedback that makes the group as a whole *feel* certain that it is making the right choice. Members discourage each other from looking at the flaws in their thought process.

Or groups may become polarized, with members shifting unreasonably to a more extreme position or clinging to opposite sides of an issue. Progress toward a rational decision thus becomes impossible.

"How could we have been so stupid?" demanded John F. Kennedy after his administration's invasion of Cuba had been soundly defeated at the Bay of Pigs. Former Yale University psychologist Irving Janis notes that the planners of this operation included some of the smartest people in America: Robert McNamara, Douglas Dillon, Robert Kennedy, McGeorge Bundy, Arthur Schlesinger, Dean Rusk, Allen Dulles, and others.

They didn't fail because they were stupid. They failed because *they followed a poor process in arriving at their decisions*. They allowed the group's internal cohesiveness and loyalty to dominate the decision-making process. Ideas that conflicted with the group's preconceptions got little attention.

Decision Trap Number 7:

Group Failure—Assuming that with many smart people involved, good choices will follow automatically, and therefore failing to manage the group decision-making process.

Groupthink

The Kennedy policymakers have plenty of company in their errors. Janis has shown that similar mistakes were committed in the decisions that led to:

— U.S. underestimation of Japan's belligerence before Pearl Harbor;

— the U.S. invasion of North Korea during the Korean War;

— U.S. mismanagement of the Vietnam War, and

— the Watergate scandal.

The best-documented examples of group blunders are found in the public sector because public officials must leave more information available to researchers than corporate executives. But we know that General Motors' creation of the ill-fated Corvair was another striking example of group bungling. A similar process seems to have occurred within the National Aeronautics and Space Administration and Morton Thiokol, the manufacturer of the space shuttle's rocket boosters, leading to the explosion of the shuttle *Challenger* in January 1986.

Upon analyzing such catastrophes, researchers discovered common elements that—though apparently innocent—seemed to lead toward tragedy:

1. *Cohesiveness*. Members knew and liked each other and wanted to preserve the group's harmony.

2. *Insulation*. Errant groups were often making decisions so secret they could not discuss their progress with outsiders.

3. *High stress*. The importance of the decision, its complexity, and tight deadline put group members under great pressure.

4. *Strong directive leadership*. The head of the group clearly stated up-front what he or she favored.

All these factors work together to create what is now called **"groupthink."** The name comes from the title of a book by Janis, which analyzed and documented the errors these groups committed. Cohesiveness, insulation, and stress generally led the groups to reach consensus too quickly, often supporting whatever their leader had initially advocated. The groups then focused almost exclusively on information that confirmed their opinions. "We've got it licked," members would in effect tell each other.

Groupthink causes otherwise capable individuals to blunder. Janis' symptoms of groupthink include:

- **self-censorship** by members, who avoid speaking up against the majority opinion for fear of ridicule or because they do not want to waste the group's time. In a memorandum, Arthur Schlesinger had stated that he considered the proposed invasion of Cuba immoral. But he kept his mouth shut when he attended meetings of the Kennedy team.

- **pressure exerted on people inside the group who disagree with the majority opinion.** Robert Kennedy, then

148

attorney general, took Schlesinger aside after learning he had opposed the invasion in writing. Kennedy said: "You may be right or you may be wrong, but the President has made his mind up. Don't push any further."

- **an illusion of invulnerability.** When Admiral H. E. Kimmel, commander at Pearl Harbor, was told that his staff had lost radio contact with Japanese aircraft carriers, he made light of the situation: "You don't know where the carriers are? Do you mean to say that they could be rounding Diamond Head [at nearby Honolulu] and you wouldn't know it?" In fact, the carriers really *were* approaching Diamond Head and had ceased radio transmissions to avoid detection.

- **erroneous stereotyping** of people outside the group. Johnson advisers during the Vietnam war took a cliché-ridden view of "the Communist apparatus" that led to a sloppy domino theory ("If we don't stop the Reds in South Vietnam, tomorrow they will be in Hawaii . . .").

The end result in every case was that too few alternatives were examined and too few objectives were taken into account. The decision frame or policy alternative first put on the table was usually adopted whether it was good or bad. Intelligence-gathering was one-sided, especially concerning the risks inherent in the group's preferred option. (Decision-makers at times failed to read intelligence reports that would have shown key assumptions to be false.)

Conformity Affects Most Groups

Even when a group doesn't face a full-blown case of group-think, many group decision processes still suffer from people's tendency to conform to group norms instead of speaking their minds. Groups need some conformity to function. If a group contains people with different conflicting frames it may achieve no agreement at all. Confusion about frames wastes vast amounts of time in corporate committees.

But it's equally dangerous for group members to withhold valuable judgments. A classic experiment demonstrating this phenomenon was conducted in 1956 by Solomon Asch. He showed people four lines like those in Figure 2. At left is the "test line"; others are labeled A, B, and C.

Each subject was asked whether the test line was equal in length to line A, B, or C. When people are asked to do this individually, over 99 percent get it right. Only people with very poor vision (or under the influence of drugs) could miss.

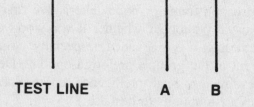

TEST LINE   **A**   **B**   **C**

Is the test line equal in length to A, B, or C?

Figure 2
THE CLASSIC ASCH EXPERIMENT

But what happens if you are standing in line behind one other person who answers incorrectly before your turn comes? In the Asch experiment, the people preceding the subjects in line were actually Asch's research assistants. The research assistants were instructed to give the wrong answer: Line A.

When one person before the subject says "A," the error rate jumps from 1 to about 3 percent. If two people in front of the subject both say "A," 13 percent of the subjects also say "A." When three or more persons ahead of the subject say "A," the error rate rises to 33 percent. And if the people in the lineup are told that a monetary reward for the group as a whole depends on how many members in the group get it right, then 47 percent of the subjects give the wrong answer.

If the desire to conform can change these simple judgments, it's not surprising that other people can influence what you say on a truly complex issue. Two heads in theory are better than one, but people often influence each other in ways that prevent the full benefit of their *independent* ideas from being realized.

How to Manage Group Decisions

Making an intelligent **metadecision**—deciding how to decide—is probably even more important in group decisions than in individual decision-making. While an individual who has started in the wrong direction can turn around and go back to square zero fairly easily, a group that realizes it is moving in the wrong direction will have a tougher time undoing agreements and expectations among members in order to change course.

Before beginning any major group decision process, therefore, the leader should ask the metadecision questions listed in Chapter 1 (page 7), plus the following two group metadecision questions:

151

—What should I use this group for?

—In which of the four key elements of the decision process (framing, intelligence-gathering, coming to conclusions, and learning from feedback) should the group participate? What is the role of the group as a whole in each one of these phases?

Figure 3 on the next page illustrates different profiles of how groups can approach a decision.

In groupthink, the group moves quickly to a consensus. Groupthink is not always bad. If the group really does not have time for extended discussion, and the leader is fairly sure of a solution to the problem at hand, then groupthink can unite the team behind a decision. In the brief discussion, members can simply add ideas that may help them to implement it.

When a sales team gathers to discuss its strategy for the week, for instance, the leader need not get each member's ideas out on the table. The team should reach a consensus quickly, end the meeting, and start selling.

In important decisions, however, groups must avoid the dangers of conformity, polarization, and group overconfidence. Wherever the leader wants the group to contribute, he or she should seek divergent thinking. That means the leader should:

—withhold his or her own ideas at first;

—encourage new ideas and criticisms;

—make sure that the group listens to minority views.

Japanese companies have an interesting custom that may be worthy of emulation: As a rule, they let the lowest-ranking member of a group speak first, then the next lowest, etc. That way, no one is held back by fear of differing with an opinion a superior has already expressed.

152

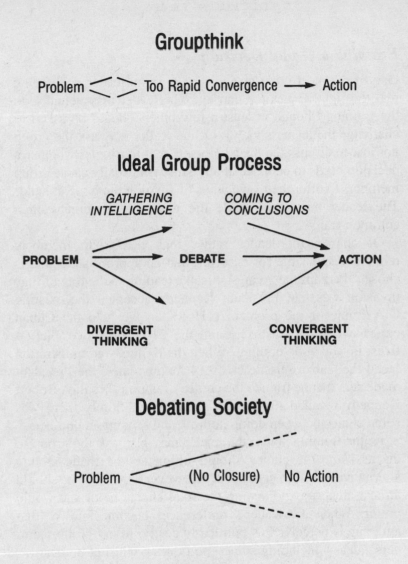

Figure 3
THREE GROUP DECISION PROFILES

153

Framing a Group Decision

One of the most important jobs of a group leader is ensuring that the right frames are chosen. The leader may actually do the framing (though at least a few others should be asked to challenge the leader's view). Or the leader may ask the group not just to discuss the decision itself, but to discuss whether a decision needs to be made at all. This will usually cause group members to offer their own ways of framing the issue at hand. The leader must then guide the group to agreement on a common frame.

Of course, the leader rather than the group members remains responsible for ensuring that an appropriate frame is chosen. Perhaps the greatest mistake leading to the Bay of Pigs invasion was that President Kennedy accepted the existing CIA frame of the problem ("How can we help the Cuban exiles overthrow Castro?") and the CIA's only two alternatives: invade or do nothing. When the Kennedy administration faced the Cuban missile crisis 14 months later, the President made sure that he framed the choice of options broadly. Robert Kennedy recalled his brother's thinking: "Surely there was some choice between doing nothing and sending in bombers."

At the framing stage, the leader may also ask the group to discuss *how* the choice should ultimately be made among alternatives to be generated. However, the leader should almost always avoid stating the final choice he or she would prefer. When the leader's preferences become known, disagreeing is perceived as politically costly. Many group members' ideas—including some good ones—will not be heard.

Group Intelligence-Gathering

The entire team usually gets involved in intelligence-gathering. Divergent thinking is central to excellent group intelligence-gathering. Encourage people to think as widely as possible, coming up with as many crazy ideas as they can imagine.

Probably the biggest barrier to outstanding group decision-making is the misconception that "conflict is bad." *Conflict (among ideas) is necessary and valuable* if a group decision-making process is going to accomplish more than simple groupthink. When it takes place in an atmosphere of mutual respect, conflict leads to higher quality forecasts and estimates. In the words of the philosopher John Dewey:

> Conflict is the gadfly of thought. It stirs us to observation and memory. It instigates to invention. It shocks us out of sheeplike passivity, and sets us at noting and contriving. . . . Conflict is a *sine qua non* of reflection and ingenuity.

To Create Constructive Conflict, Create Heterogeneous Groups

Healthy conflict occurs most in groups:

—whose leaders understand the need for well-framed questions,

—that have heterogeneous members, and

—that use processes designed to delay forming an early consensus.

To maximize the diversity in a group, select team members who differ both in background and in thinking style. If members think about problems in many different ways,

155

they're more likely to produce conflicting ideas. Thus they're more likely to teach each other something, and conflict between them will lead to new insights.

Even if a decision seems to call exclusively for computer experts, for instance, try to include some marketing or accounting people on the team.

At the same time, you need to manage the group to ensure that you have conflicts among ideas, not conflicts among personalities.

Mixing Personalities

Many leaders achieve adequate diversity in decision-making teams simply by choosing people who strike them, intuitively, as approaching decisions in differing ways. Also, many psychological tests exist to help analyze personality differences, and some may be especially helpful in putting together decision-making groups.

One such test, for example, is the Myers-Briggs personality inventory, which asks a series of questions that seeks to classify people on different "dimensions." Two of the dimensions are particularly pertinent to decision-making, namely:

1. to what extent people screen or filter information that they receive (i.e., receptive versus focused), and

2. to what extent people arrive at final conclusions via analytic thought versus via gut feel (i.e., thinking versus feeling).

The "receptive" types have a good eye for detail, and like to absorb many facts. A receptive manager who favors a thinking (rather than feeling) mode tends to be hard-nosed and practical. Examples include Harold Geneen (former head of ITT) and Robert McNamara (former head of Ford and former Secretary of Defense). Geneen would say, "Facts are the

156

highest form of professional management." Not surprisingly, he created a control-oriented management team that ran ITT by the numbers (and was greatly feared by those less well versed in facts and figures).

In putting together a work group, try to know which of your people are naturally better with facts versus concepts, and who depends more on gut feel as opposed to analysis. Then mix them up, so that a sound portfolio of cognitive skills is put to work for your important, complex issues. Don't assume that "thinking" people consistently do better in business than "feeling" people. (For example, "feeling" people in one test were able to decode a ciphered message while members of a "thinking" group could not.) "Feeling" people may be particularly strong at exploring diverse frames or grasping a big picture. But "thinking" skills are often needed when it comes to a careful choice among clear alternatives. What is important is to recognize how different people have unique strengths and weaknesses that can complement each other. Well-managed task forces balance these different skills.

The next box highlights some of the decision characteristics of different orientations. Sometimes people with differing orientations may not work together well at first. Their styles will conflict (as the box shows). But complex problems usually require multiple approaches. And often the extra conflict these style differences cause is well worth it.

Many companies routinely have employees take the Myers-Briggs test or another, similar psychological evaluation. You may want to obtain the scores of potential team members before making your final selection.

Processes to Prevent Premature Consensus

Another helpful step to encourage healthy conflict is to create subgroups. Often leaders break intelligence-gathering teams

157

DECISION STRATEGIES OF DIFFERENT TYPES

Receptive types tend to:

> Suspend judgment and avoid preconceptions.
>
> Be attentive to detail and to the exact attributes of data.
>
> Insist on a complete examination of a data set before deriving conclusions.

Focused types tend to:

> Look for cues in a data set.
>
> Focus on relationships among the facts.
>
> Jump from one section of a data set to another. So as to develop some explanatory structure.

Thinking types tend to:

> Look for a method and make a plan for solving a problem.
>
> Defend the quality of a solution largely in terms of the method.
>
> Define the specific constraints of the problem early in the process.
>
> Move through a process of increasing refinement of analysis.
>
> Complete any discrete step of analysis that they begin.

Feeling types tend to:

> Redefine the problem frequently as they proceed.
>
> Rely on unverbalized cues, even hunches.
>
> Defend a solution in terms of fit.
>
> Consider a number of alternatives and options simultaneously.
>
> Jump from one step in analysis or search to another and back again.

into subgroups to focus on different jobs. But it may be especially revealing to create two different subgroups for the *same* job. They're sure to come up with different perspectives on the issues at hand.

Also, try assigning someone to be devil's advocate at each group meeting. Even a weak dissenter will help. When in the earlier Asch experiment just one subject out of seven gave the right answer (line B), the error rate dropped from 33 percent to just 6 percent.

One warning: don't designate the same person as the devil's advocate all the time (and try to discourage any one individual from falling into that role). The group will just learn to ignore him or her.

You can also require that each individual offer at least two alternative views on each major issue. That prevents anyone from being too closely identified with (or taking too much pride in) a single view.

In addition, group leaders can bring about productive conflict through the techniques of brainstorming, lateral thinking, and synectics—which we discussed in Chapter 3 (pages 46–47) as part of our discussion on reframing and creativity.

Mutual Respect in a Group That Argues

People can battle other group members and still maintain mutual respect *if* the organization teaches its people to:

> Be critical of ideas, not of people.

Several techniques can help ensure that members of groups maintain mutual respect.

—At one of the group's first meetings, the leader can go around to each group member and explain "why I

159

selected you." This is an opportunity to recount past contributions of each member.

—The leader can make sure that each person gets to speak on all key questions.

—The leader can ask someone on one side of an issue to further develop a point made by someone on the other side. For example, if a meeting involves conflict between the design and the manufacturing departments and a manufacturing person says that components should be designed so they won't break in the assembly process, you might ask a designer to elaborate on how that might be done.

When groups can achieve the ability to cooperate even when members disagree sharply, they become excellent problem solvers. To illustrate, consider the following accounting puzzle:

A woman buys a $78 necklace at a jewelry store. She gives the jeweler a check for $100. Because he does not have the $22 change on hand, he goes to another merchant next door. There he exchanges the woman's check for $100 in cash. He returns and gives the woman the necklace and her change. Later the check bounces and he must make it good to the other merchant. He originally paid $39 for the necklace. What is his total out-of-pocket loss?

When this problem is assigned to individuals, the majority become confused. In our experience, only about one third of managers get it right. But when groups tackle it, members catch each other's errors. Group members argue (often heatedly), but they usually come up with the right answer. In one study, 60 percent of the groups working on the problem got it right. More important, virtually every group in which mutu-

160

ally respectful conflict emerged eventually found the right answer. (The correct answer, incidentally, is sixty-one dollars. A simple way to solve it is to use an accounting frame: List revenues and expenses.)

Conflict and mutual respect are the keys to excellent group decision-making.

The Final Choice in a Group

When the intelligence-gathering phase for a major decision is complete, the evidence on the table should be rich enough that no one feels his or her views were ignored.

The entire group can now focus on developing a systematic approach to choosing, such as the subjective linear model discussed in the last chapter. Group members may disagree on the weights that should be assigned to different factors. But all members should at least feel that the weights the group ultimately favors—and which will determine the final choice— were chosen reasonably. Ideally, everyone should agree that a good decision process was followed, even if he or she disagrees with some of the inputs.

Sometimes, however, strong disagreements will persist. People may radically dispute some of the estimates arrived at during intelligence-gathering. Or they may disagree vigorously on the weights assigned to factors in the decision. Some may even believe that a factor that others consider a reason *not* to take a particular step is really a reason the step *should* be taken. (For example, if the question in a manufacturing business is whether to remain in a niche that faces unpredictable foreign competition, many executives may consider such competition a clear reason to pull out. Others may feel that learning to meet that kind of competition is vital to the entire business's long-term future.)

When fundamental disagreements persist, the group should

161

~~seek to separate~~ the factual judgments and assumptions underlying each side's position from ~~their value judgments.~~ It should challenge each assumption, get further data (using an outside expert if necessary) to reduce or eliminate the continuing factual disagreements, then try to generate new alternatives that will better fit both sides' values.

Uniting the Police and Its Critics

This approach is perhaps most useful in creating decisions that will satisfy people who have opposing interests in a complex policy question.

Traditionally, political systems have dealt with policy issues dialectically: One side advances its arguments and the other side does likewise. A third party tries to reconcile or find the truth in the conflicting viewpoints. (This adversarial approach is especially used in the judicial process.)

Unfortunately, this method is costly (like war). Moreover, it polarizes the two sides.

Often, better approaches exist. The city of Denver, Colorado, for example, managed to reconcile police and minorities who held opposing views by separating factual issues from value issues on a contentious topic: A proposal that police be equipped with more powerful bullets.

The issue flared up when police realized they were facing a major threat to their lives: After police shot fleeing suspects, the suspects often retained enough strength to get up and shoot back, wounding—and in at least one case killing—an officer. The department wanted to switch from traditional, lightweight bullets to a new, hollow-tipped bullet that would stop suspects more reliably.

Minorities and the American Civil Liberties Union were outraged. They declared that the new bullet would kill or maim innocent suspects and bystanders.

Each side employed ballistics experts to testify in favor of its proposed bullet. But that generated only vituperation. In the adversarial process, experts become hired guns. The one-sided experts were adding little to the city council's understanding.

A New Framework

The city council thus turned to Professor Kenneth Hammond of the nearby University of Colorado, a behavioral decision expert. Hammond set out to separate the factual opinions of people involved in the issue from their value judgments. He used a framework of the type shown in Figure 4. The left side contains the objective characteristics of various bullets, defined in a scientific manner. For example, bullets differed in their muzzle velocity, their weight, their shape, etc. These could all be objectively measured.

Unfortunately, these easily measurable characteristics meant little to politicians, minorities, or even officers of the police department. Members of minority groups might have a general feeling that heavier bullets were more dangerous than lighter ones. But their real concern was for the variables shown in the next column: Injury potential, threat to bystanders, and stopping effectiveness. Only experts in ballistics and medicine could determine how muzzle velocity, weight, shape, etc., actually led to injury potential, threat to bystanders, and stopping effectiveness. Hammond realized (and convinced the Denver city council) that experts respected by both sides should make the scientific judgments about how each bullet would score on these dimensions.

Hammond also emphasized, however, that once the scientific judgments had been made the experts possessed no additional qualifications for the value judgments that would ultimately determine which bullet the city should select. The value judgments were essentially choices about how much weight to put on each of the factors in the second column. The final choice, Hammond said, should be based on both the scientific judgments about each bullet and a set of policy weights (shown as W_1, W_2, etc.) that assign a relative importance to each factor. The city council, as representatives of the public, should choose the weights.

It turned out that the ballistics experts who testified for the police and the ballistics experts who testified for the minority

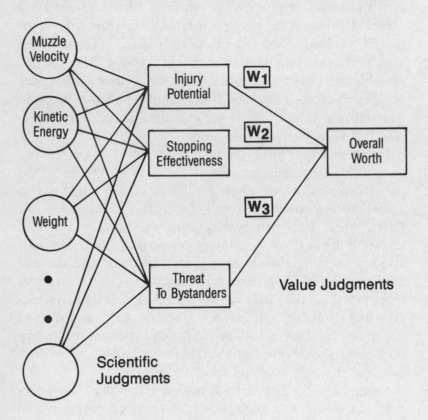

Figure 4
RESOLVING THE BULLET CONFLICT

164

groups differed little in their scientific judgments. They had previously favored different bullets only because they differed in their personal value judgments.

But Hammond found that once he consulted ballistics and medical experts outside an adversarial atmosphere, they could add a great deal to the debate. A panel of ballistics experts and doctors told the city council that bullets with the greatest injury potential might not have greatest stopping effectiveness. A bullet that produced a relatively small, shallow cavity when it hit the body would produce less injury than a bullet that produced a long, wide, deep cavity. Yet some bullets that produced small, shallow cavities nonetheless had considerable ability to render a suspect shot in the torso incapable of returning fire. Hammond's group asked the experts to make scientific judgments on some eighty different bullets.

The issue of how to weight these judgments was emotionally charged. City council members could not be expected to assign the subjective policy weights dispassionately if they were asked to do so directly or publicly. To ascertain the policy weights, Hammond asked the decision-makers to give hypothetical judgments among dozens of bullets which were described only in terms of their stopping effectiveness, injury potential, threat to bystanders, etc. Indeed, some of these test bullets were hypothetical; they did not exist.

His group then derived implicit weights for stopping effectiveness, injury potential, etc. Next they applied the city council's value judgments to the scientific findings concerning the eighty or so bullets that were real options.

The conclusion: The bullet that had the highest overall score was neither the old bullet the police department had been using nor the new bullet the police department had proposed. It was a bullet that had not previously been considered.

It was nearly equal in stopping effectiveness to the bullet the police department had originally proposed. However, it presented no greater potential for injuring suspects or bystanders than the bullet the department had been using.

A good decision process had succeeded in meeting both sides' key goals.

Other Uses of Separating Facts from Values

Separating facts from values is generally a good technique to deal with complex, emotionally charged issues such as gun control, anti-terrorism measures, environmental controls, drug testing in the workplace, etc. For example, someone opposed to a gun control proposal might be asked what data would be convincing enough that the benefits outweighed the costs.

If the person would under no circumstances favor gun control, then we know that the issue is to this individual exclusively a question of values. If, on the other hand, the person would favor control if there were sufficient statistical evidence that it reduces violent deaths, then the debate can shift from just values to evidence.

We used this technique in helping the father we introduced on pages xiii–xiv decide among three conflicting medical recommendations regarding his daughter's hip deformity. The technique also has its uses in business. The Harris Trust and Savings Bank in Chicago recently applied it to their computerized trust systems. Much money and time had been invested in a custom-designed information system, but opinions were strongly divided on whether to continue. To prevent emotions from dominating this complex decision, management hired a consulting firm (Touche Ross) to coordinate the evaluation of the in-house system and compare it with three integrated systems available from outside vendors. Four criteria were used: (1) cost, (2) timeliness, (3) operating features, and (4) risk.

A surprising consensus emerged on how each of the four

166

systems scored on each of the policy criteria. Next, a senior management group was asked to prioritize the four policy criteria (by distributing 100 points among them). These weights were then applied to the four systems. The in-house system was outscored by at least two of the external vendors' systems. The gap was big enough that fairly strong agreement could be reached on discontinuing development of the existing in-house system.

Surviving in a Mismanaged Group

Unfortunately, we all must deal with decision-making groups that are not really well managed. How can you survive in a group that isn't well run?

The basic rules are:

1. Understand the leader's frame (especially his or her goals).

2. Try to communicate what you believe the group needs to do to make a good decision.

3. Be tactful and positive. The goal is to highlight the reservoir of insight that lies dormant in the group, not necessarily to "convert" your boss or your fellow group members.

If the leader is highly directive—that is, he or she is anxious to act like a "boss"—you should probably speak to him or her privately about the decision process. First, analyze the boss's frame, so you can try to speak in its terms. Make an agenda listing what you want to say. Focus on the decision process and if necessary supply articles or other authorative sources on group management. You may not be able to convert a bossy leader into a good listener, but you can improve communication and maybe help the boss get more from the team.

If the boss is not highly directive but just confused, make your points publicly but diplomatically. Ask whether the group's purpose is to brainstorm and challenge or just to fill in details in a decision that is already largely made. (Your company may have a legitimate reason for limiting the group's role, and even if it doesn't, your career won't benefit from undermining the boss's point of view.)

Ask where the group is in the phases of decision-making. Does the leader have a clear frame? Are we seeking to get many ideas out on the table for good intelligence-gathering? Or does the leader think it's time for convergence and a final choice?

If the leader or the group as a whole is receptive, suggest procedures to prevent the formation of a premature consensus: The creation of subgroups or of a rotating "devil's advocate" role.

Conclusions: Managing Conflict for Excellent Group Decisions

Generally, the art of helping groups make better decisions can be summarized as follows:

1. Intelligent, well-motivated people make superior decisions in groups *only* if they are managed with skill.

2. The heart of good group management is encouraging the right kind of conflict within the group, and resolving it fully and fairly through further debate and intelligence-gathering.

3. Leaders must decide where in the four elements of a decision (framing, intelligence-gathering, coming to conclusions, and learning from past cases) the group can make its greatest contributions.

4. Leaders should rarely state their own opinions early in the group's deliberations, because many group members will fear to offer their own (possibly good) ideas if they contradict the leader's.

5. Generally, leaders should encourage disagreement in the early stages of any group process. Then as more facts and insights are gained, the leader should guide the group toward convergence on a final choice.

6. If a decision process really deadlocks, you can often narrow the gap by separating factual issues from value issues.

Groups can make better decisions than individuals, but only if they are helped along by a skillful leader. There is little excuse for using costly group meetings to make inferior decisions. Unfortunately, this is what often happens.

Part IV

====

LEARNING FROM EXPERIENCE

====

Chapter 8
Why People Fail to Learn

People sometimes stumble over the truth, but usually they pick themselves up and hurry about their business.
WINSTON CHURCHILL

One of the oldest and largest lotteries in the world is the Spanish National Lottery. Participation is a Spanish obsession. The lottery runs every week, but the Christmas drawing is by far the largest. The entire event is televised and the winners become celebrities overnight. To emphasize that the process of choosing winners is incorruptible (i.e., purely random), young boys from a Madrid orphanage draw the winning tickets.

One grand prize winner was asked by the Spanish news media: "How did you do it? How did you know which ticket to buy?" He replied that he had searched until he found a ticket ending with the number forty-eight. When asked "Why forty-eight?" he responded: "For seven nights in a row, I dreamed of the number seven, and since seven times seven is forty-eight . . ."

This story is delightful. The winner doesn't know how to multiply, and he certainly doesn't know he's claiming credit for an event that happened through the purest chance. He has fallen victim to what is called the "illusion of control." People often exaggerate the extent to which they control events. When events come out well, self-aggrandizement further biases them to see the success as the result of their own genius. But if events turn out badly, they face an equally pernicious bias toward rationalization—creating an explanation of the bad results that preserves their positive self-image.

In addition to these two biases produced by our *desires*, people also suffer from hindsight effects caused largely by the way our minds work. We are often unable to reconstruct how we thought about an issue before we learned its outcome, and thus we may fail to draw the appropriate lessons even if we carefully prevent ourselves from rationalizing. Overcoming these biases makes learning from experience a more difficult task than most people realize.

Experience Is Inevitable; Learning Is Not

In this chapter we'll examine the biases that cause us to misinterpret our experiences and how to overcome them. Then in the next chapter we'll discuss how you can improve and more realistically analyze the feedback you receive. If you understand your biases, know how to create good feedback, and can interpret feedback realistically, you can consistently turn your experiences into reliable knowledge—perhaps for the first time. And that can make the difference between advancing steadily throughout a long career and repeating the same mistakes over and over again.

Learning from experience isn't automatic. It requires profound skills. Experience, after all, provides only data, not knowledge. It offers the raw ingredients for learning. And people can turn it into knowledge only when they know how to evaluate the data for what they really say.

People do not learn as easily from experience as you might expect—even intelligent, highly motivated people. A study of clinical psychologists, for example, demonstrated that capable professionals failed to improve their skills even after years of experience using a standard diagnostic technique.

174

In a careful experiment, experienced psychologists and two less experienced groups of people tried to diagnose whether patients were suffering from brain damage using the standard Bender Visual-Motor Gestalt test. In the Bender Gestalt test, patients are shown figures (such as partly overlapping circles and triangles) and asked to draw them by hand. Research has shown that if certain features are present in the hand drawings (e.g., disproportionate overlaps or missing intersections), the patient is likely to suffer from brain damage. But the relevant symptoms can be hard to recognize. The test cannot be easily scored by computer; a psychologist has to judge whether truly significant distortions are present. And surprisingly, the performance of the experienced psychologists suggested they'd learned little about interpreting patients' drawings from years of administering the test.

The three groups compared in the experiment were

1. psychologists with many years of experience using the Bender Gestalt test.

2. graduate student trainees, who had an average of roughly three years of experience with the test, and

3. the secretaries of the experienced psychologists, all of whom were familiar with the terminology of the test but had no experience or training in actually interpreting patients' drawings.

Each group was presented with a series of drawings patients had produced. All the patients had later gone through further diagnostic tests, so the scholars conducting the experiment knew which of the drawings were really produced by brain-damaged individuals.

How did the groups compare?

—The experienced psychologists correctly determined whether the patients had brain damage 65 percent of the time.

—The graduate students were correct 67 percent of the time.

—The secretaries were correct 70 percent of the time.

In other words, the psychologists diagnosed brain damage less accurately than their secretaries. Somehow they had learned little from years of testing and working with patients.

Note that we are not talking about indifferent or unintelligent people. These psychologists cared enough to participate in a study even though they knew it might produce unflattering results. Their problem was an inability to turn their experience into improved knowledge. In contrast, one renowned expert who specialized in the Bender Gestalt test achieved 83 percent correct, higher than anyone else studied. He had succeeded in learning because he had found ways to systematically process feedback from patient after patient to improve his skill. But when the other psychologists failed to focus on learning, little learning occurred.

Claiming Credit

Although we congratulate ourselves for our great actions, they are not so often the result of great design as of chance.
LA ROCHEFOUCAULD

Why don't people learn from their experience? For one, the data we receive can usually be interpreted in more than one way. And even when the evidence is clear enough that we should be able to learn from it, we are naturally biased to interpret it in a way that preserves our positive self-image.

The story of the Spanish lottery is a dramatic example of the confusion between skill and chance. Yes, the winner *did* make a careful choice, and yes, he *did* win the prize. So why

176

shouldn't he believe that his own wisdom caused the success? Because in this case, it is unambiguously clear that the underlying process was truly random.

However, once there is even a slight component of skill in a victory (as in almost all professional settings), it becomes extremely hard to acknowledge that a success is due primarily to chance rather than genius. Yet only by recognizing the role of chance in successes can you realistically learn which of your actions you should carefully repeat and which could be improved. Falsely claiming credit is an important barrier to learning.

We all need to feel that we have some control over our environments. Feeling powerless is debilitating. Experiments have shown that dental patients who are told they have the power to flick a switch and turn off the drill, for example, remain more relaxed and happy than similar patients to whom no such control is granted—even if the people with the switch never exercise their power.

In another study, two experimental groups of workers were made to endure the same distracting background noise. Members of one group, however, were informed that they could turn off the noise at any time. Although they never touched the control switch, the group with control performed better than the group that had no control.

Unfortunately this need for control distorts our perception of reality. It causes us to overestimate the odds of success and lay the wrong bets. In June 1983, the National Basketball Association (NBA) held its annual player draft to assign the right to negotiate with each player about to graduate college. The prize in the 1983 draft was seven-foot-four Ralph Sampson of the University of Virginia. The two teams with the worst records in each of the NBA's two divisions would decide who would have first choice (i.e., the right to pick Sampson) on the basis of a coin flip. Here's what a manager of the Indiana Pacers—

177

one of the two teams—said shortly before the coin flip: "We're going to win it. Somehow, some way, we're going to do it. We seem to be on a roll right now."

And there is good reason to believe that the Pacers' management believed what they were saying. The other eligible team, the Houston Rockets, had made an attractive offer to the Pacers for their half of the coin flip. (The offer was the number-three pick in the 1983 draft, Houston's first pick in the 1984 draft, and the Pacers' choice of one of two established players on the Rockets' current team.) A Pacers representative said about the offer, "We turned it down . . . We're perfectly content to go into the coin toss, stare them right in the eye, and flip."

On May 19 the coin was flipped. Houston won. The Pacers had passed up a good deal because of an illusion.

Such illusions of control frequently cause us to repeat actions that in the past were followed by success, even if there's no reason to believe the actions did anything to cause the success. In the early nineteenth century, European settlers in what is now Iowa encountered a tribe of Native Americans who subsisted almost entirely on the buffalo, which wandered about in large herds. Whenever the buffalo moved far away, the people faced starvation. In response, braves would perform an elaborate buffalo dance continuously, night and day, some replacing those who dropped from exhaustion, until the buffalo returned. Eventually the buffalo always returned, and the tribe interpreted this as proof of the dance's effectiveness.

How many activities similar to buffalo dancing exist in modern organizations—from corporate planning rituals to superstitions about how to prepare for big events? The illusion of control and accompanying false claims of credit for good outcomes are firmly rooted biases to allay our deepest fears about an uncontrollable world.

Decision Trap Number 8:

Fooling Yourself About Feedback—failing to interpret the evidence from past outcomes for what it really says, either because you are protecting your ego or because you are tricked by hindsight effects.

Rationalization

While people eagerly overestimate their control when planning an action and when looking back on an action that has turned out well, most people also possess a genius for underestimating their errors when looking back on an action that turned out badly. To avoid the pain of admitting mistakes, we rationalize. We may:

—distort our memory of what we actually did or said;

—unrealistically blame the failure on others or on supposedly unforeseeable circumstance;

—say our original prediction was misunderstood or misinterpreted;

—change our current preferences so the failure seems less important (for example, after being fired career success may become less important to you).

Self-serving explanations often seem natural, entirely plausible. They make what seems dissonant coherent again. But rationalizations benefit us only in the short-run. You can learn from mistakes only if you acknowledge them. So rationaliza-

179

tion extracts a heavy price: We suppress the most important disconfirming evidence of our careers, perhaps the most valuable information we will ever receive.

One Rand Corporation report, for example, documented cost underestimates on new energy plants. The average overrun in ten projects was 153 percent. The managers responsible blamed factors entirely outside their control, from bad weather to changes in government regulations. Yet the Rand report showed that 74 percent of the cost-estimating errors could be traced to foreseeable, preventable causes.

Of course, the managers' rationalizations may have been partly aimed at improving their chances of obtaining future jobs. But they surely learned less from the experience of underestimating costs than they could have. (If you really must give your boss a misleading rationalization of why a project has failed, at least note down what you would do differently the next time in a file the boss won't see. But rationalization is usually driven by our internal needs, rather than any real need to impress others. Most often, bosses will recognize that a balanced appraisal of the good and bad points of your actions shows you are dealing realistically with errors.)

You Can't Have It Both Ways

Because we like to believe that we caused successful outcomes and we like to rationalize that we weren't responsible when things turned out badly, most people suffer from an attribution bias that can destroy useful feedback. In short, we believe that:

Our successes are due to skill, our failures to bad luck.

This may be the most pervasive of all self-serving interpretations of experience. It is not for nothing that the Duke of Wellington said, "Victory has a thousand fathers; defeat is an orphan."

One study examined the chief executive's letter to share-

180

holders in annual reports of eighteen large corporations over a period of eighteen years—three hundred and twenty-four letters in all. They found that management claimed credit for 83% of the positive events while accepting blame for only 19% of the negative events. We found similar results when we looked at private divisional reports in a large corporation. Clearly, someone is fooling someone else in that company.

Avoiding Self-Serving Explanations

> *The empiricist thinks he believes only what he sees, but he is much better at believing than at seeing.*
> GEORGE SANTAYANA

What can you do about your bias toward claiming credit for your successes and rationalizing away your failures? First, you need self-discipline—the willingness to be as objective as possible. Acknowledge that some mistakes are inevitable and indeed necessary (like dry holes in the oil-prospecting business). The person who never makes mistakes is unlikely to accomplish much.

Then, try these approaches to accurately separate your real mistakes from chance events:

—clearly set criteria or milestones beforehand that unambiguously define success or failure, or else perform a goal analysis—explicitly listing the outcomes you personally want or dread—to flag those outcomes you will be least able to judge objectively in hindsight.

—specify beforehand to what extent you believe your own choices can influence the outcome of your effort.

—ask other people who had nothing to do with the project how much of your success or failure they think you should credit or blame on the actions you took. (before and after learning the results).

—for repeated decisions (personnel choices, new product introductions, advertising investments, etc.), see if a statistical test can be conducted to determine the role of chance vs. the role of wise choice in the outcomes.

—periodically list your failures; if the list is short, be suspicious. Ask others (who are not too dependent on you) to augment the list.

—carefully analyze how the new information from the outcome of a recent project should cause you to revise a scenario you already prepared for a future project. (If you're in charge of new locations in the Northeast for a retail chain, for instance, and you learn that some company-owned stores somewhere else have dropped precipitously in value, study how events that caused the price decline elsewhere might affect the scenarios you've created for the Northeast. Construct your scenarios as we suggested in Chapter 5, pages 110–111.)

Hindsight

Every great scientific truth goes through three stages. First people say it conflicts with the Bible. Next, they say it has been discovered before. Lastly, they say they have always believed it.

LOUIS AGASSIZ,
nineteenth-century biologist

We all know the false clarity of hindsight. Events may seem inevitable in hindsight, even though they might have been very hard to predict beforehand.

To some small extent, we may actually understand a

situation better when we think about it in hindsight. (See Chapter 5, pages 111–113, for the discussion of prospective hindsight.) But in general, the clarity of hindsight is an illusion. And it often hampers learning from experience. Like claiming credit falsely for successes and rationalizing mistakes, the false clarity of hindsight creates the illusion that there is no lesson to be learned.

But more than the dangers of the other biases, the dangers of hindsight can't be avoided by mere willingness to be objective. They are not solely rooted in our wishes, but also in the mechanisms of our mind—which are largely beyond our rational control. They demand that we take steps to prevent the ill-effects when we first make our decisions.

A study by Baruch Fischhoff and Ruth Beyth demonstrates the strength of the hindsight bias. Prior to Richard Nixon's trips to China and Russia in 1972, they asked students to consider fifteen possible outcomes such as:

—the U.S. will establish a permanent diplomatic mission in Peking, but not grant diplomatic recognition;

—President Nixon will meet Mao Tse-tung at least once;

—Nixon will see Soviet demonstrators;

etc.

The students were asked to assign a probability to each possible outcome. Then after the trip, the students were asked in hindsight to assess the likelihoods of these various outcomes and also asked to remember or reconstruct their original probabilities. When the interval between the two tests was just two weeks, 67 percent thought their original estimates were closer to the truth than they really were. For example, the remembered probability that Nixon would meet Mao was higher in hindsight than that actually given before the trip (because students knew that Nixon indeed had met Mao). When a four-to-eight-month interval had elapsed (and fewer people could actually remember their original probabilities), 84 percent showed the hindsight bias.

Why do such hindsight effects exist? We want to make sense of the world. Part of the hindsight bias may simply result from our need to feel that we knew what was likely to happen. But probably a larger part is a result of the way our minds process information. Our minds are not filing cabinets that store information the way it came in. Instead, we edit the information heavily, cut it up into pieces, and file the edited extracts in multiple parts of our minds, depending on what they are associated with. We synthesize and integrate new information into old knowledge. Like a glass of red wine poured into a bowl of clear water, the new blends with the old. Thus, it becomes impossible to reverse the process. We truly cannot think the way we did before we knew that Nixon met with Mao during his Chinese trip. Similarly, adults cannot draw pictures as they did when they were four years old. (Even if adults draw stick figures, they use elements of perspective and proportion that kids acquire only later.) We can't easily undo what we have learned.

Note the depth of the problem this creates for learning from feedback. Do the results of the China trip call for a reevaluation of the students' prior view of China or of Communists? Do they suggest reevaluating China as a business partner? To judge accurately, the students should compare what they've learned with the assumptions that underlay their previous opinions. But they can't do that if they can't recall or reconstruct their earlier views.

"Nothing Really New"

Hindsight can make people miss the significance of important analysis as well as make them misunderstand events. Thus it can hurt people who act as advisers or consultants. One manager responsible for computer simulations of marketing strategies regularly received one of two responses to his simulation reports: Either

"We already knew that," or

"This is so implausible that your model must be wrong; go back and check your assumptions."

The manager couldn't win. When his boss had finished reading his reports, his most useful insights appeared obvious because of hindsight effects. The simulation manager finally moved to another position in frustration and disgust.

We call this the **"Nothing-really-new problem."** If your boss's best guess about an important value—say expected market share—is 10 percent then the hindsight bias will make all values near 10 percent seem useless. If your report predicts a market share of 12 percent, the boss will feel that she knew it all along. In fact, the more convincing your report is, the more your boss will feel that she knew your prediction all along.

If your prediction is 40 percent, on the other hand, you're in trouble again. It is so far from the boss's intuition that her probable response is disbelief.

Often people who think the boss's interpretation is wrong must produce a report that differs just enough from the boss's prediction—say, forecasting 17 percent when the boss's prediction is 10 percent—that the boss can see a surprise without getting a shock. At 17 percent, you stand a reasonable chance of being recognized for good work.

But the best solution to the "Nothing-really-new problem" is to ask people to predict or guess in advance what you found before they read your report. Then you can demonstrate just how your analysis differs from their initial assumptions. Or in a presentation, ask the audience to write down its views prior to your revealing the new information. That way you will most impress them with the value of what you have learned. Without such precommitment, people will probably say they knew your discoveries all along (and really believe that).

The hindsight phenomenon is one reason you should record important agreements of all kinds in writing. This is something lawyers are carefully trained to do, but not other professions. Without a written record to turn to, people naturally come to believe different versions of the same fuzzy agreement once new information arises. Moreover, they may have strategic reasons to misremember.

Understanding hindsight also tells us how to present past business events when training junior executives: Don't present the outcome with the case. Make the trainees decide what they would have done in the same situation. This will convey the difficulty of the original decision and the uncertainty of the outcome. If junior managers get the outcome with the case, the real flavor of the decision will get lost in a "knew it all along" feeling produced by hindsight.

What can you do about the hindsight bias? There's no instant solution. In experiments, careful warnings about the dangers of hindsight effects don't seem to help people much.

The key is prevention rather than cure. A judgment diary to record your current predictions and opinions can minimize hindsight effects.

Make yourself and your subordinates record, say, their predictions for the success of a new branch office, or predict in writing how a new person will work out, or how a negotiation will progress. This will prevent self-serving interpretations where people claim that they knew right from the start that the product or branch office would fail. Wouldn't such a record make a fascinating document? With personal computers integrated into an office network, such decision diaries become even more feasible.

Creating a full diary may consume more of your time than it's worth. But when you make a major decision, you should certainly write down not just the decision itself, but the rationale behind the decision. Only by keeping some kind of record—and referring back to it from time to time—can you ensure that you will realize when you have something to learn. Most people who do this are often surprised how much their thinking has changed (as when reading a childhood diary).

Conclusions: Overcoming Your Internal Barriers to Learning

The biases we've discussed in this chapter are key reasons why people don't learn as much as they could from experience.

Slow learning can ruin you or your organization in a rapidly changing environment. While in science new learning may take hold only slowly (until an entire generation dies out), competitive businesses can't afford such a long wait. Fortunately, you can minimize the biases we've discussed if you remember the dangers and work to overcome them:

—Don't fall into the trap of *claiming credit* for successes that have occurred by chance. When you succeed at something, honestly consider which of your actions seem to have contributed to your success and which probably didn't. Ask others to help you in your evaluation.

—Avoid *rationalization* when you fail. If you exaggerate the importance of bad luck in your failures, you miss one of the biggest opportunities in all of professional life: The chance to learn from the failures that you'll inevitably experience. When you receive feedback from previous decisions that displeases you, discuss its importance with others. Review scenarios you've created for the future and decide whether they should be changed.

187

—Minimize the effects of the *hindsight bias* by keeping records of what you expected when you made your major decisions. Then compare the real outcomes to the expectations, and consider what lessons you *should* learn.

Simple steps can go a long way toward helping you learn. Unfortunately, however, the purely mental barriers to learning that cause us to protect our egos or fall into hindsight traps aren't the only problems that keep people from growing wiser through hard experience.

To a large extent the world seems to conspire against learning. Often we get no feedback at all on the outcomes of our decisions, or we get partial or misleading feedback. The combination of the internal biases we discussed in this chapter plus the poor feedback most of us receive make real learning a truly challenging endeavor (and for most people, a regrettably rare event). In the next chapter we'll discuss strategies to cope not only with our internal biases, but with the ambiguous and often misleading nature of real-world events.

Chapter 9
Improving Feedback

Experience is a good teacher, but she sends in terrific bills.
MINNA ANTRIM,
*Naked Truth and
Veiled Illusions, 1902*

In the last chapter we discussed three major biases that keep us from properly interpreting feedback: our desire to claim credit for successes, our desire to rationalize away our mistakes, and the distorting effect of hindsight on our memories. These biases make learning difficult, even when experience provides clear feedback.

Unfortunately, as we will show in this chapter, experience usually provides feedback that is far from clear. There are, however, steps you can take to make the most of the evidence experience provides.

Often the results of your actions remain unknown. If you approve the research department's request for a budget increase, for example, it may take years before the results of your action are known. By then, you may be elsewhere in the organization and you may never learn whether the department did anything useful with the money.

Or ambiguity masks the relationship between your action and the eventual outcome. You can't always tell whether you did right or wrong, even if you do manage to avoid rationalizing. (For example, suppose the research department *did* discover something useful after you increased their budget.

189

Can you tell whether the increase was responsible for the discovery? Or might the discovery have happened anyway?)

To learn consistently, most people need not only to understand their own biases, but also to improve the quality of the feedback they receive. In this chapter we will show you how to recognize inadequate feedback and augment it. We'll also show how to learn from experience even when you can't get good direct feedback on the effects of your decisions.

What's Wrong with the Feedback We Get Now?

To improve the quality of the evidence experience gives us, we should start by understanding what's wrong with the feedback we're receiving today. Then we can watch for opportunities to overcome each of the major problems.

Most people's experience is afflicted by:

—missing feedback: a lack of information on key questions;

—entwined feedback: evidence is affected by actions taken by the decision-maker and associates *after* making the initial judgment;

—confused feedback: uncontrollable, unpredictable factors— "random noise" that affect decision outcomes;

—ignored feedback: incomplete use of the information on outcomes they already possess.

Missing Feedback

Much of the information that would be most useful to us is simply unavailable. For example, we can learn about the success or failure of the job candidates we hire but we usually learn nothing about those we reject. If you refused to hire

Applicant X, you'll never know how well X would have done in your organization.

Look at Figure 5. Suppose that each year, sales force applicants are accepted (or rejected) according to some decision policy meant to select those who are most likely to succeed in sales. Let's say that 200 people apply for 100 positions. Later, the performance of the 100 hirees is evaluated, as shown on the vertical axis. Suppose 50 are successful and 50 are not.

What do these data tell us about the quality of the selection rule? Not much. We don't know what would have happened to the 100 rejected applicants. Perhaps 50 of the 100 rejected applicants would also have succeeded. Then the rule for deciding who is likely to succeed is worthless. But ordinarily

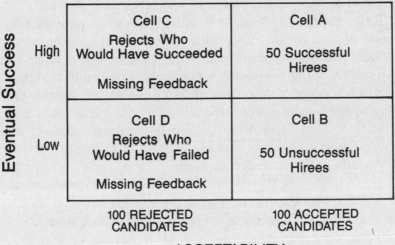

Figure 5
THE PROBLEM OF MISSING FEEDBACK

191

you'd never learn that crucial fact. (Note also that you can make your "success rate" lower or higher just by changing your criterion for success.)

Treatment Effects: Entwined Feedback

Often we and our coworkers influence the outcomes of our decisions in ways that make the quality of the decisions themselves hard to judge. When senior managers choose protégés, they do much more than bet on the protégés success; they also tell their protégés they believe in them and do many other things to increase the chances of their protégés success. The company that accepts 100 of 200 applicants doesn't just select them; it also puts them through a training program. Although such actions make good sense, they confound later attempts to analyze the outcomes and learn from them.

Researchers call these confounding factors **treatment effects.** A "treatment" is anything done after a judgment that influences the outcome. A common form of treatment effect is the **self-fulfilling prophecy:** a prediction that comes true not so much because of the quality of the prediction but because of actions by someone who believed in it. Such outcomes are usually desirable. But the cost of increasing the likelihood that they will be achieved is that you distort your feedback.

An article in *Bartender* magazine, for instance, offered a guide to predicting big tippers on the basis of the drinks they order. The best tippers are supposed to order Scotch or vodka on the rocks, or bourbon or cognac straight. Those who order Grasshoppers, Pink Squirrels, or Brandy Alexanders presumably are more parsimonious.

But waiters who are trying to predict potential big tippers are likely to give expected big tippers exceptional service. They think, "Why waste my time on cheapskates?" Not surprisingly, these preferred customers tend to leave the bigger

192

tips. Is it because the waiters accurately spotted good tippers, or is it simply because they gave some customers better service?

Or consider the effect of a training program. A company training program may take recruits who had a 50 percent chance of succeeding and improve their success rate to 80 percent. But all the personnel managers will know is that 80 out of 100 new members of the firm succeeded. Managers cannot know from such statistics whether the success rate is due to

1. a very good hiring rule (followed by a worthless training program);

2. a superb training program (that more than compensated for mediocre recruits selected by a useless decision rule); or

3. some combination of a sensible rule and an effective training program.

Treatment effects often go unrecognized, posing even greater damage to learning. Bosses may not realize that they or their secretaries are favoring a protégé. Supervisors may not realize that they are examining the work of subordinates they distrust more closely than the work of others, and that this is the real reason they find more errors in it. Employees often don't know they're shunning handicapped, less educated, or other workers they consider inferior. Bartenders don't always realize they're neglecting those they consider cheapskates.

A classic study of elementary school teachers illustrates how a prophecy can subtly fulfill itself. Teachers were told that some of their pupils were "late bloomers," i.e., that the results of a recently administered test showed them to have great potential for improvement. In fact, these students had performed neither better nor worse than the rest of the class on

193

the test. The only thing special was their teachers' belief that they had untapped potential.

Nonetheless, the "late bloomers" were soon outperforming the rest of the class. Somehow the teachers caused the unfounded prophecy to be fulfilled. (We know that when teachers believe students to be bright they are more likely to maintain eye contact, to smile, to nod their heads, and to give other nonverbal indications of approval.)

Perhaps self-fulfilling prophecies are nowhere more common than in job interviews. Interviewers form impressions from reading job applications, then find confirming evidence when they conduct the interviews. In one study, interviewers were told (randomly) that personality tests revealed the person they were about to interview was either warm or cold. Sure enough, after the interview they described the interviewee exactly as they had been led to expect.

Not all treatment effects lead to self-fulfilling prophecies. A treatment may undermine the trend the forecaster predicted, for instance. If a financial analyst says that a bond will sell for a lower price than is justified by its payment stream, for example, his forecast is likely to cause bargain-hunters to bid the price of the bond up, making the forecast inaccurate. But self-fulfilling prophecies are a very common form of treatment effects in business.

Random Noise: Confused Feedback

Even where treatment effects are unimportant, the data we receive often do little to prove a decision right or wrong. The outcome of almost any decision is affected by what scientists call random noise: uncontrollable and unpredictable factors.

If you contemplate opening a new hamburger restaurant, for example, you can't be expected to anticipate such events as bad weather in the year you open, government reports that discourage people from eating hamburger, or an unexpected recession. You can't take credit if your restaurant becomes popular because it sold a million-dollar lottery ticket, if the newspapers write about it because a movie star stopped there, or if a strike hits a nearby competitor.

These latter factors are mostly random noise. The presence of random noise enables people to rationalize away failures and claim credit for successes they did little to produce. But people can also blame themselves for failures caused by random factors and deny themselves credit for successes that were caused by a combination of luck *and* a great deal of skill. If you make the same kind of decision many times (hiring salespeople, for example), the random factors probably average out and they don't affect your long-term success *rate*. But we make most of our most important decisions only once or at most a few times in our lives. No matter how wise you may be, "noise" greatly complicates learning from single or isolated experiences.

Poor Use of Existing Information: Ignored Feedback

In addition to suffering from missing feedback, random noise, and treatment effects, most people overlook or even destroy a good deal of information that could help them understand whether their decisions have been wise and how they might be improved in the future. The new product manager at one company told us:

> "Never have we performed an experiment to see whether those products we decided not to produce would have succeeded or failed." ◐

That is missing feedback.

Then he added that his company closely evaluates for national marketing purposes only those products that appear successful in initial market tests. It does not attempt to determine why the other products failed the initial tests. The company accumulates considerable information in initial test marketing about how consumers really think. But part of that feedback is systematically ignored.

Neglected and misused feedback are very common. We know of a consultant hired by a nonprofit social agency to help it get more grants. The consultant began by trying to understand what characterized a successful grant application. He went to the agency's files only to find that all the agency's unsuccessful applications—about 90 percent of all applications—had been destroyed.

People often ignore important feedback about their failures because feedback about successful decisions seems somehow more important to them. Look at Figure 5 again. It is the *successful* applicants (Cell A) that we prefer reviewing. Cell A (which corresponds in the case of the social service agency to the successful grant applications) appeals to our penchant for confirming evidence (see Chapter 5) and our desire to claim credit for successes. Even where information corresponding to all four cells is available, the natural appeal of Cell A causes most people to focus on the successes.

Where information about the other cells is unavailable—or where a little bit of analysis and rummaging in the files would be required to make it available—people rarely take the trouble to fill it in. Consider the person who says, "I can always tell when somebody is wearing a hairpiece." This individual may remember the many times he or she has recognized someone wearing a hairpiece. However, the person may never have considered how many people wear hairpieces that escaped notice.

A catastrophic example of neglected feedback was the data regarding O-ring failures in the space shuttle boosters prior to the disastrous flight of the *Challenger* on January 28, 1986.

196

Technicians had studied the O-rings after each of thirty earlier space shuttle flights. For seven of those flights, they had discovered serious wear. Engineers were vaguely aware that these instances seemed correlated with cold weather. When they learned that NASA intended to launch the *Challenger* despite temperatures in the thirties, they objected.

But the positive feedback from twenty-three successful launches had made top NASA officials overconfident. The worried engineers were asked to graph the temperatures at launch time for the flights in which problems had occurred. The result appears in Figure 6. The top officials weren't impressed. Several problems had occurred in flights at temperatures of 70 degrees or higher. Top managers at NASA and Morton Thiokol (the rocket booster's builder) agreed that evidence on whether cold temperatures caused O-ring problems was "not conclusive." They okayed the launch. The O-rings failed and the rocket exploded, killing all aboard.

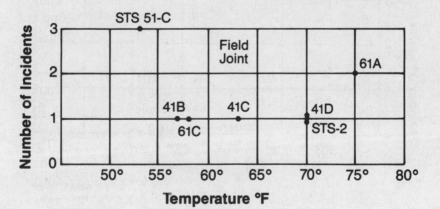

Figure 6
DATA REVIEWED PRIOR TO LAUNCH

In reviewing the decision to launch, Figure 7 was produced. It is the same as Figure 6 except that it also includes data showing the temperature at launch time for all flights in which *no* wear on the O-rings was discovered. Every one of the flights on which the O-rings escaped damage took place at a temperature of 66 degrees or above.

Properly managed feedback would have shown that cold weather enormously increased the chance of O-ring failure. Not only should the top managers have been more sensitive to the data, but the engineers who knew problems were correlated with cold should have known that they needed to prepare a chart like Figure 7. Of course even the engineers who strongly felt that cold temperatures could cause problems

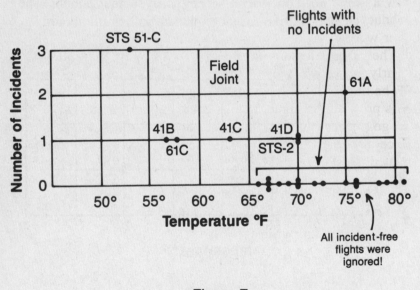

Figure 7
THE FULL STORY FROM PAST FLIGHTS

might have had difficulty introducing evidence that would undermine the organization's self-image of invulnerability.

A Regular Learning Analysis

A regular learning analysis is a key step in fighting missing feedback, treatment effects, random noise, ignored feedback, and other natural biases. In a learning analysis you address the question, "What have I learned [and what should I be learning] from recent experiences?" It forces you to draw reasonable conclusions, imprints the lessons of your experience in your mind, and enables you to plan strategically for learning in the future.

Generally a learning analysis should start with a meeting between a boss and a few associates (though there's no reason why a group of junior analysts with no one under them can't conduct its own learning analyses, perhaps starting over a beer after work).

The biggest lessons of the last few months may hit you clearly between the eyes when you start to look for them. ("The market is no longer price sensitive. . . ." "Company X is producing a higher quality product than we are. . . .") To go deeper, the basic question of what you have learned since the last audit should be supplemented with several related questions:

1. What have I learned about my own frames?

2. What have I learned about the way we gather intelligence for our decisions?

3. What have I learned about the process by which we reach final conclusions around here?

4. In general, are we happy about our decision processes?

199

In addition, questions about barriers to learning should be addressed, including:

1. Which of my lessons did I learn naturally in the course of my work? Which did I learn because I made a specific effort to learn them?

2. What additional feedback would improve my learning? For instance, suppose I had kept more thorough track of all my beliefs, estimates, predictions, etc., throughout the decision process. What information would I now seek from this record to learn as much as possible from what has actually happened? Should record-keeping systems be changed so I can find this information in the future?

3. Are we making appropriate use of information the organization has been retaining (such as memos from past decision processes that are kept on file)? Are any of our existing record-keeping requirements unnecessary?

4. How much could our competitors be learning about me, my decisions, or my organization if they set out to study us systematically? Am I neglecting any information that would be freely available to them? (For example, do you know what your customers *really* think about you?)

The conclusion of a project may be a natural time to conduct a learning analysis. If you make decisions continually (for example, if you are a loan officer, or a personnel manager), the analysis can be conducted once or twice a year—perhaps at the same time as standard performance reviews.

All organizations should institutionalize learning and regular learning analyses. British Petroleum, for instance, has a powerful unit at corporate headquarters that does nothing but analyze major recent decisions for lessons applicable to the company as a whole. (We shall return to this in the next chapter.)

200

Require your staff to devote time to intelligence-gathering to permit future learning about today's decisions. Change company policy to retain, analyze, and report the most important types of feedback on past decisions. Performance evaluations could include questions like, "How much analysis of past decision processes did the employee engage in?"

The structure and frequency of the learning analysis should depend on the particular situation. But everyone needs some form of learning analysis at regular intervals.

Decision Trap Number 9:

Not Keeping Track—Assuming that experience will make its lessons available automatically, and therefore failing to keep systematic records to track the results of your decisions and failing to analyze these results in ways that reveal their key lessons.

Experimentation: Designed Feedback

Can you improve feedback beyond simply retaining better records and analyzing them more carefully? The answer is yes: For instance, you can obtain better feedback by conducting experiments.

Look back at Figure 5. In principle, you can obtain the missing feedback about hiring decisions by conducting an experiment in which all 200 applicants are accepted (or, more likely, in which the 100 available slots are filled with 50 regular accepts and 50 who would have been rejected). In this way, you can obtain the full feedback for one year and use it to judge the quality of the decision rule. To test not only the effectiveness of your hiring rule but also the significance of the "treatment" given by a training program, you could give 25 of the 50 who would normally have been accepted the regular training program and put the other 25 to work without any training (or with less expensive training).

But are such experiments worthwhile? Often the idea of such experiments seems crazy. Personnel managers spend their lives trying to recruit the best possible people. They may feel they're neglecting their duty if they hire people they consider inferior.

From this one-year experiment, however, you will learn how good your decision rule really is and how to build a better one. Then in all succeeding years you can select employees more effectively. In other words, if the experiment teaches you anything useful, the success rate of the people you hire should increase as soon as the better decision rule can be used.

Thus, you face a trade-off between short- and long-term goals. In this light, accepting rejects no longer seems so crazy. It may still be too costly to run the full experiment. But the decision should be based on a cost/benefit analysis that includes the estimated long-term benefits. For instance, you may want to try a smaller experiment—perhaps accepting 20 people who would otherwise be rejected.

Some Real Experiments

The IRS uses a strategy like this. Each year it carefully audits those taxpayers it believes are most likely to have seriously underpaid their taxes. However, the IRS appreciates that its decision rule for identifying underpayers is never perfect. A resourceful public, aided by former IRS agents who write books about escaping detection under the current rules, is

202

always trying to avoid tax audits. To recover this year's underpayments and at the same time build a better rule for detecting next year's likely underpayers, the IRS uses a two-pronged strategy. It follows a carefully crafted rule to select most of the people it audits. But it also audits a smaller random sample of tax returns.

The Bell System offers another compelling example of the value of experimentation. As regulated monopolies, Bell System operating companies cannot refuse service to new customers—even those they believe are poor credit risks. However, the companies are allowed to cover these risks by requiring a deposit from a predefined percentage of customers. Thus the companies want to identify those new customers who are most likely to default, and then require deposits from exactly those people. The importance of an optimal decision policy for deposits is magnified by the size of the Bell companies, with 12 million new customers per year. Before the 1984 break up of the system, the total bad debt was over $450 million per year.

But the Bell operating companies had turned for advice to the famous Bell Laboratories, which suggested an experiment. Nearly 100,000 randomly selected new customers were given telephone service without a security deposit. This bold action was certain to cost a lot of money in defaulted payments, but it would probably help to build smarter selection rules.

But how much smarter? Would the new savings, if any, be worth the cost? After nine months the results of the study were in. New decision rules were built, one for each of the fifty states. Bell Laboratories estimated that these more intelligent decision rules would save it $137 million per year, every year for at least a decade. The experiment itself probably cost less than one-tenth of that.

Note that the revenue increase was not obtained by requiring more deposits. The reduction in bad debt was achieved solely

203

by more intelligently identifying the high-risk new customers, based on more complete feedback. The phone companies required deposits not from *more* customers, but from *different* customers.

In his memoirs, advertising executive David Ogilvy exemplifies the experimenting spirit. To stay a step ahead of his competition, Ogilvy pursued a strategy of trying a few novel, offbeat ads, ones that typically would be rejected under standard decision rules and that "conventional wisdom" predicted would fail. Indeed, most of these ads did flop; however, the few that succeeded proved extremely profitable and pointed the way to innovative approaches. What's more, the flops were not that costly. Ogilvy watched his "experiments" closely and quickly pulled the losers. The benefits of discovering new advertising approaches clearly outweighed the costs of "accepting rejects."

Experimentation can likewise solve entwined feedback problems caused by treatment effects. What, for example, could waiters do to find out if their "big tipper" decision rules are any good? They should give equal service to all customers, regardless of the expected tip. This eliminates the treatment. Then, at the end of the night, they can see whether the predicted big tippers actually left bigger tips without the inducement of better service. If they did, the waiter's decision rule is valuable. If not, it's worthless.

But can waiters really control themselves in the service they give? Might the service given unconsciously be affected by who they *think* is a bigger tipper? A more scientific experiment would be conducted "blind." A senior waiter could tell three junior waiters the information in *Bartender* magazine (that the biggest tippers order scotch or vodka on the rocks, or bourbon or cognac straight). Then tell three other junior waiters exactly the opposite: That the biggest tippers order Grasshoppers, Pink Squirrels, or Brandy Alexanders and the worst tippers order scotch, vodka, bourbon, or cognac and, after a few nights, compare the actual totals of tips.

Although waiters' tips may seem a trivial example, this kind of experiment has importance for many big organizations. Customer service is a major expense in most businesses, and in most companies people hold strong—but sometimes erroneous—beliefs about how to allocate scarce service resources. Feedback from the field is unclear. But well-constructed experiments—in which salespeople call regularly on customers who had not been considered worthwhile, for example— may discover vital information for the company.

Statistical "Experiments"

Suppose you can't (or don't want to) conduct an experiment that involves deliberately violating your existing rules. Is there any other way of gaining meaningful feedback?

Yes. You can conduct a statistical analysis that tests whether your assumptions are realistic. For example, suppose you want to test whether your hiring decision rules are well founded without actually hiring anyone you deem to be inferior.

Your current decision rule takes account of your applicants' sales experience, their education, the impression made during an interview, etc. Are these really factors that predict sales success in your company?

If they are, then not only should the people you hired perform better than those you did not hire, but those who scored *best* in the applicant pool should perform better than those who scored just barely high enough to be hired. Do they? Look at their records and find out.

You can't get as full or complete an account of what factors predict success in sales through this kind of statistical analysis as you can by hiring a random sample of applicants. But you may well demonstrate that some factors you considered important don't predict success at all.

Process vs. Outcomes

Sometimes you can't get direct feedback on the outcome of a decision, or if you can it won't arrive in time to do you any good. Or the outcome in a particular case may be determined as much by chance (random noise) as by the quality of your decision.

In these cases, you have to focus not on learning from outcomes but on learning through analysis of the decision process itself. Indeed, where outcomes are dependent on both your decision and on chance, the feedback from reviewing your decision process may help you far more than the feedback from reviewing outcomes. So in general, a careful review of decision *processes* is a vitally important part of obtaining feedback on your decisions.

Many managers can't learn from studying decision processes because they are irrationally wedded to judging anyone favorably who achieves a good outcome. Consider the following problem:

Someone is faced with a choice between two coins, each of which will yield $0 if tails comes up or $1 million if heads comes up.

Coin A has a 50 percent chance of success (heads).

Coin B has a 60 percent chance of success (heads).

Naturally the person chooses Coin B. Now suppose that both coins are flipped. Coin A turns up heads but Coin B turns up tails.

Did this person make the right decision?

We posed this problem to managers and asked them to rate the quality of the decision on a scale from 1 (clearly made the wrong decision) to 7 (clearly made the right decision). Their average rating was 5.1.

The correct answer is that the decision was absolutely correct. It deserved a 7. If you disagree, ask yourself the question, "If the game were played again, which coin would I choose?" Universally people choose Coin B, the one with the higher probability. This shows that, despite the poor outcome, they believe the original decision was the right one.

So let's focus on the decision process. On what basis should a coin be chosen? You want the coin with the higher probability of success. So of course Coin B is superior. The optimal decision rule is simple: Choose the coin with the higher probability of success. But chance confuses the link between good decisions and good outcomes.

Let's consider the same problem in a business context.

Imagine your company must choose to market one of two potential new products. Assume that you know with certainty that product A has a 50 percent chance of succeeding, while product B has a 60 percent chance of succeeding. In both cases, success means the same thing—a profit of $1 million. If either product fails, however, your company will receive nothing. The company chooses to market product B. Product B fails, but product A is later marketed by a competitor, and it succeeds. Did the company make the right decision?

A second group of managers was given this business version of the coin-toss problem. Their average rating on the 1 (wrong decision) to 7 (right decision) scale was only 4.4 (compared with the 5.1 for the coin-toss case). In other words, managers were *less* clear on the rightness of choosing the alternative with the higher probability of success when the problem was posed in a "close to home" business context.

Yet the company made the right decision just as clearly as the coin flipper. Our managers' judgment was influenced by the outcome even when they knew that the outcome was the result of random factors.

Only when managers realize that they need to create processes that maximize the likelihood of success and separate out chance factors as much as possible can they reasonably evaluate subordinates or learn appropriately from their own experience. Of course you can never separate out chance factors completely—it's likely that the junior executive whose territory booms will rise faster than the junior executive whose territory slumps, even if the cause was pure chance. But at least looking for a good or bad decision *process* will dramatically increase the chance that you and your company will do well in the long run.

U.S. manufacturers in numerous industries have sometimes found, for instance, that some Japanese companies have brought new technologies to market quicker—and in forms that customers have liked better—than U.S. firms. There seemed no reason to believe that the Japanese were any better engineers than the Americans, and no easy generalizations could be made about the specific Japanese design decisions. (The products ranged from photocopiers to auto engines.) It seems that the problem was that the Japanese had more systematically analyzed the *process* of design. They were spending the time necessary at early stages of the process to understand both the capabilities of existing technology and the needs of users. Then they would produce a simple basic design. And they had organized the process of converting basic design to salable product, including all the minor decisions that had to be made in that process, much as they had earlier organized the process of manufacturing. They had gotten the *process* of design decisions right.

Lord Mansfield advised:

Decide promptly, but never give any reasons. Your decisions may be right, but your reasons are sure to be wrong.

The clever lord recommended that you never reveal your reasoning (i.e., your decision process) because it might prevent you from taking credit for successful (but purely lucky!) outcomes. In other words, play the organizational game so as to be able to make good luck look like great skill.

Most people are promoted for good outcomes—the traditional bottom line—not necessarily good decision processes. But today, following Lord Mansfield's advice in business is generally not enough to advance your career. People who merely make a few lucky decisions and try to rationalize away their mistakes are unlikely to rise as far as people who learn by reviewing their decision processes. You may sometimes work for a boss you can manipulate with a strategy like that, but to make a great career honestly, you need to develop an excellent decision process.

Good bosses, in fact, should have a strategy that will defeat young Lord Mansfields. They should encourage you to reveal, document, study, and continually improve your decision processes.

Summary

Learning from experience is especially difficult when you face an uncooperative environment—i.e., when there is missing feedback or ambiguity due to random noise or treatment effects. Unfortunately, that's exactly what most people face most of the time.

To improve with experience, therefore, you need to:

—regularly *analyze what you've learned* recently and how you could be learning more;

—conduct *experiments* to obtain feedback you could get in no other way; and

—learn not just from the *outcomes* of past decisions but also by studying the *processes* that produced them.

Chapter 10
Changing Your Way of Deciding

At the day of judgment, we will not be asked what we have read, but what we have done.

THOMAS A KEMPIS,
The Imitation of Christ, 1420

Throughout this book we've tried to provide tools and concepts to improve your decisions. They can dramatically enhance almost anyone's work performance.

But experience has shown that even when readers know they're getting good advice, books may change their behavior only slightly. Readers of books rarely benefit as much as those working under live coaches where pupils get highly specific advice, tightly focused on their particular errors. Although this book contains the same suggestions that we would give you in person, you may miss or neglect the most important steps to improving your particular decisions.

We want our advice to avoid that fate. We want you to make better decisions. So in this chapter we will discuss how to conduct a decision audit.

In a decision audit, you should analyze your own decision-making and identify a few key steps *you* ought to take to dramatically improve *your* decisions. Once you've located the few crucial errors, you'll find that your decision-making can be improved much more easily.

211

> ## Decision Trap Number 10:
>
> **Failure to Audit Your Decision Process**—failing to create an organized approach to understanding your own decision-making, so you remain constantly exposed to all the other nine decision traps.

Start by Reevaluating Your Use of Time

Start your decision audit with the Decision Phases Worksheet on the next page. As we discussed in Chapter 1, we ask managers at the end of our seminars to evaluate in which of the phases of decision-making they've spent what share of their time in the past. Then we ask them how they want to divide their time in the future and how, being realistic, they expect to. This gives a basic indicator of how each individual wants to change the decision process.

(If you deal mainly with group decisions, the "coming to conclusions" phase should include all periods when the group is gathering information to resolve disagreements among group members. As "intelligence-gathering," count only time spent gathering data and comparing notes aimed at encouraging group members to "diverge" and bring out more ideas.)

After you've filled out the worksheet, ask yourself what barriers hinder a proper allocation of time. How can they be removed?

For example, are you under pressure to *pretend* you have fully framed the question before you really have given framing

212

DECISION PHASES WORKSHEET*

	What share of your time did you devote to each phase in the past?	What share of your time do you intend to devote to each phase in the future?
1. Framing		
2. Intelligence-Gathering		
3. Coming to Conclusions		
4. Learning from Experience		
	100%	100%

*Distribute 100 points within each column to reflect your actual and intended time allocations.

adequate thought (perhaps because your boss doesn't understand the importance of careful framing)? Do you have enough time for intelligence-gathering? Are your records too poor to permit proper learning from feedback?

Here are typical time allocations from the managers we talk to. Note the increased emphasis on framing and learning. Managers often say that intelligence-gathering and coming to conclusions are not less important, but that with a good decision frame part of this effort can be delegated to others.

Phases	Actual Time Allocation	Intended Time Allocation
Framing	5%	20%
Intelligence-Gathering	45%	35%
Coming to Conclusions	40%	25%
Learning from Experience	10%	20%

Auditing Your Decisions

After you've evaluated your use of time, list several recent decisions on a separate sheet, including:

—at least one decision in which you achieved good results because you followed a good decision process, and

—at least one decision in which you suffered bad results because of a poor decision process.

Choose one good decision and fill out the Decision Evaluation form on the next page. The Decision Evaluation form asks you to grade yourself (A, B, C, D, or F) on how well you avoided each of the barriers we have highlighted in our ten

214

DECISION EVALUATION

The decision:

Decision Traps	Grade*	Benchmark Private	Professional
1. Plunging In	＿＿	2.6	2.0
2. Frame Blindness	＿＿	2.6	3.0
3. Lack of Frame Control	＿＿	2.7	2.9
4. Overconfidence in Your Judgment	＿＿	2.5	2.7
5. Shortsighted Shortcuts	＿＿	2.7	2.9
6. Shooting from the Hip	＿＿	2.5	2.8
7. Group Failure	＿＿	2.9	3.0
8. Fooling Yourself about Feedback	＿＿	2.8	2.9
9. Not Keeping Track	＿＿	2.5	2.6
10. Failure to Audit Your Decision Process	＿＿	2.2	2.3

If your decision was a success, what was the key problem you needed to overcome?

If your decision was a failure, what was the key trap that caused you to err?

Did other problems or challenges arise that are not included in our list of the ten most common traps?

*Evaluate here how well you managed to avoid each trap by giving yourself a "grade" (from A to F). For comparison we have listed the average grades (on a four-point scale) that 130 Chicago MBA students gave themselves for managing and avoiding these ten traps in their private and professional decisions.

Decision Traps. If you think that some of these barriers did not apply to your particular decision, simply write "N.A." (not applicable) under "Grade." Finally, write down what you think was the key problem you overcame to make this decision well.

Next, make a copy of the Decision Evaluation form, and fill it out for a poor decision. At the bottom, write down the trap that caused you to fail.

You can now go on to the Personal Decision Audit sheet that follows if you want. But you may want to fill out Decision Evaluation forms on several more decisions. After you've filled in about four or five, however, you should start trying to answer the Personal Decision Audit. You may still be unable to answer fully. Feel free to go back and fill out Decision Evaluation forms on a few more decisions if you have time or if you don't feel you can complete the Personal Decision Audit fully. The more Decision Evaluation forms you fill out, the less your conclusions on the Personal Decision Audit will suffer from availability biases.

Team audits can also be highly effective. Your work group can meet to complete both the Decision Phases worksheet and the Decision Evaluation form. Such group exercises offer two big advantages. More people means more perspectives and less rationalization. And people are often more motivated in groups to do a thorough job—even in a group of just two.

The Benefits of Personal Decision Audits

We've asked many students and executives completing our course to conduct decision audits. The results have been impressive.

In one case, for example, a personnel manager at a nonprofit organization evaluated a good decision (to hire an

PERSONAL DECISION AUDIT

1. List the frames you typically use or favor.

2. List the heuristics (rules of thumb) you typically employ.

3. List your preferred strategies for arriving at final conclusions.

4. List the barriers to learning (both internal and external) that affect you most.

5. Which phase of the decision process do you find most problematical? Which decision traps are most dangerous for you?

6. Which of the problems you have identified do you think you can solve merely by being aware of them?

7. Which will require specific actions (changing the way you make estimates, formalizing procedures, conducting learning analyses after major decisions, keeping better records, etc.)? List the actions you should take.

8. Can you implement these steps by yourself, or must you involve others (boss, subordinates, etc.)?

9. Give yourself a "grade" (from A to F) on your average performance for each of the following aspects of decision-making. (Distinguish between private vs. professional decisions if necessary.)

Metadecision	Framing	Intelligence-Gathering	Coming to Conclusions	Managing in Groups	Learning from Feedback
___	___	___	___	___	___

10. Ask someone else (who knows you well) to complete questions 1–9 for you as well. Discuss any major differences in answers.

assistant personnel manager) and a bad decision (to hire a secretary for a key officer of the institution). She discovered how closely she had followed the decision steps when she had decided well. She learned how losing track of her decision priorities (in her bad decision process) could destroy a good frame. And the audit as a whole revealed her own key weaknesses in decision-making generally.

In the good decision, she found:

—She had made an intelligent metadecision. The personnel manager's position had been redefined—to the organization's benefit—by the previous person who held it. The administrator realized that the hiring decision should involve seeking someone like the previous incumbent rather than seeking someone who matched the former job description.

—She had framed well. Early in the decision process she had extended the frame of the problem to recognize the importance of making current staff realize they had opportunities for advancement and, since she would be seeking many applications from current staff, being meticulously careful that the applicants would feel they were treated fairly.

—She had gathered intelligence well, paying special attention to avoiding overconfidence. The inclusion of the importance of perceived fairness in the frame helped prevent overconfidence. Although she already knew the applicants, she established carefully designed criteria for the job and asked a colleague in another part of the organization to interview the top four applicants.

—She had created a well-structured system for choosing. She used a modified threshold rule to eliminate any candidate who scored exceptionally poorly on any of four

218

key criteria, cutting the number of candidates from twelve to four. Then after further interviews she had used a scoring system that was essentially a subjective linear model to make the final choice.

In the bad decision, she had started similarly. She had initially framed the decision well, emphasizing that she was searching for candidates who would keep the office running smoothly.

But in the information-gathering phase, she started to experience *lack of frame control*. She had (wisely) asked an administrative assistant in the department—who would be a coworker of the new secretary—for advice. The administrative assistant pointed out that only one of the applicants for the secretarial job said her career goal was to be a secretary. The administrative assistant said she feared the other top candidates might quit soon after being hired. Then the administrative assistant would be left with the job of helping hire and train a replacement.

The personnel administrator hadn't been impressed with the candidate who wanted to be a secretary, but she allowed the administrative assistant's goal—"get someone who won't quit"—to become dominant in the problem frame. Then when she checked references, she asked only questions that would confirm her idea that any of the three leading candidates could do a good job. In retrospect, she remembered that former bosses seemed "less than enthusiastic" about the administrative assistant's favorite candidate when they were asked "Does she get along well with coworkers?" and "Is she able to draft correspondence?" But she didn't delve further, choosing to "ignore the potentially disconfirming information."

The secretary's future boss left the final choice to the personnel manager and the administrative assistant. Rather than turn to a systematic procedure for making the final choice, the personnel manager deferred to the administrative assistant. She fell for a kind of groupthink: "I withheld my judgment in the interest of avoiding conflict," she recalled.

The administrative assistant's choice was hired. But she performed poorly. She fought over "turf" with others (including the administrative assistant) and she couldn't draft letters the boss was willing to sign.

This decision audit showed that groupthink could operate even in a group of two—and that it could cause problems even when the person expressing the ill-considered, premature opinion was lower in rank than the other member of the group. That might not be an important danger in many institutions, but it was an important discovery for a personnel administrator in this particular nonprofit organization, where this kind of situation is fairly common.

The decision audit also showed the personnel manager that she was weakest in metadecisions, framing, seeking disconfirming intelligence and managing group decisions.

An Organization That Audits

Groups and whole organizations should conduct decision audits, too. A few organizations have institutionalized decision auditing. British Petroleum's system, which we mentioned in the last chapter, is excellent.

BP maintains a separate Post-project Appraisal Unit at corporate headquarters in London. It has great latitude in choosing what decisions to review (though it typically focuses on the biggest decisions, where the most is at stake). A manager and four assistants report directly to British Petroleum's board of directors.

The Post-project Appraisal Unit conducts only six project appraisals per year because the corporation "can absorb only so much information at a time," said Frank R. Gulliver, one of the unit's founders, in a 1987 *Harvard Business Review* article. The unit not only chooses its own audit subjects, but is also charged with communicating its discoveries throughout the organization.

By creating a separate Post-project Appraisal Unit, BP has encouraged objective decision auditing. (If the boss orders you to do an audit, you usually have reason to be less than candid.) Post-project Appraisal Unit members interview in pairs. One asks questions while the other watches the interviewee (for signs of doubt or less than perfect candor).

The decision-auditing system has saved BP tens of millions of dollars. For example:

—studies of two natural gas conversion plants showed one plant that came in under budget and ahead of schedule (in Australia) but produced poor returns and another that was completed over budget and a year late (in Rotterdam) but was highly profitable. The decision audit showed that BP needed much better techniques to estimate future demand in individual markets.

—studies revealed that enormous losses were being produced because project managers were approving unrealistically low budgets. The corporation adopted better cost-estimating techniques.

—studies showed BP executives' fears that they might be "beaten to the punch" in corporate acquisitions were usually overblown. They taught BP to take the time to accurately assess risks.

—studies showed BP had been losing millions of dollars because it was inadequately evaluating the capabilities of contractors before hiring them. They caused the company to create a separate unit to evaluate contractors.

221

Whether you just run a household or you run one of the world's largest corporations, decision audits can tell you how to improve your life.

Draw Your Own Conclusions

Instead of concluding this book with a sterile list of the *most* important lessons of decision coaching, we ask you to draw up a list of the most important lessons for *you* based on your decision audit. Used by themselves, the all-purpose decision-making methods we've offered in this book may be relatively weak and will solve a limited number of your problems. However, if you tailor them to *your* work, you'll find they can be extremely powerful.

From your audit, make a list of three to seven of the *biggest opportunities for improvement* in your own decision processes.

Try to fix the problems on your list over the next six to twelve months. Then do another decision audit approximately a year from now. If the improvement is disappointing, keep at it. Just as one weekend at a tennis camp does not perfect your game, one audit will not eradicate all errors. But *periodic* audits, followed by disciplined changes, inevitably will yield superior performance.

Perhaps some problems can be fixed only by helping your organization as a whole to change. That's hard, of course. Ideally, organizations should be anxious to learn and to tolerate mistakes, as long as the people who make the mistakes are working to achieve good processes. In a famous story, an executive dejectedly approached Thomas J. Watson, the founder of IBM, after making an error that had cost the company $10 million.

222

"Go ahead," said the executive. "Fire me. I deserve it."

"Fire you?" Watson responded. "I just spent $10 million educating you."

Many organizations are not run as well as Watson's, however, and we can't always make them run like that. But we can use whatever power and freedom we have within our own organizations to nudge them in the right direction. Merely focusing on what kind of processes they are using and suggesting ways to improve them can often create significant changes for the better over time.

Toward Better Decisions

The bottom line: start implementing better decision practices now, in whatever way you can. A Chinese proverb says:

> *I forget what I hear;*
> *I remember what I see;*
> *I know what I do.*

If you do not change how you make decisions, then there is a good chance you have wasted the time you've spent reading this book. A less ancient American proverb captures the essence of the Chinese in fewer words:

> *Use it—or lose it.*

Epilogue
Thinking About Thinking:
The Key to Managing in the 1990s?

Most of the information in this book comes from a relatively new discipline called cognitive science—the study of how the human mind works. However, several important trends suggest that the cognitive path means much more than better decisions. We suspect the cognitive perspective may be the single most useful approach to management success in the 1990s.

The Cognitive View

What is the cognitive perspective? Haven't psychologists always studied how our minds think about and understand the world?

To some extent yes. But cognitive science brings together fields besides psychology, such as artificial intelligence and neuroscience. Combined with stronger methods and concepts, it has achieved a better understanding of complex thinking, such as how we make decisions. The fruits of this work are only partly reflected in this book. For example, deeper insights into language and communication have led to important advances in speech recognition. And artificial intelligence programs now routinely mimic experts in such tasks as

225

designing computer systems, troubleshooting automobile engines and diagnosing certain medical problems.

Understanding how humans think—both when we think well and when we think poorly—is especially important today. A key problem for organizations today is attention management—controlling where we will devote our attention (and the attention of other professionals) to produce the results we seek. We can never marshall enough intellectual resources to address all the ever-increasing amount of information the world produces. But our growing understanding of the thinking process can help us to use wisely the limited amount of attention we can give to problems.

We believe that in the future most professionals will use the discoveries that cognitive science provides, and that the cognitive approach could be the key methodology to attack the business problems of the next decade. By understanding how good thinking succeeds and how errors are made, we can better manage both the vast quantity of information that now besieges us and the vast complexity of the modern business world.

New technologies, global competition, and environmental limits will place a greater premium on mental flexibility and sound judgment. What is a good management approach today may not be tomorrow. In our Information Age, the race will not go to the strong, but the cognitively swift.

In every decade, the main source of improved management can be characterized by a few central themes. (See box, p. 227.) In the early part of the twentieth century, the "scientific management" movement called for an analytic approach. From the early 1930s, the "human relations movement" emphasized the need to understand the psychology of work. Then, beginning with the complex logistical needs of World War II, the "operations research" movement sought to use sophisticated mathematical methods, including the application of the first electronic computers, to solve business problems.

226

MANAGEMENT THEMES THROUGH THE DECADES

1. Scientific Management (starting in early 1900s)
    Universal principles of efficiency
    Search for frictionless organizations
    The rise of industrial engineering

2. Human Relations (1930s and following)
    Hawthorne studies at Western Electric
    Psychology of work and motivation
    Participative management and job enrichment

3. Operations Research (1940s and following)
    World War II needs and the advent of computers
    Quantitative models of organizational problems

4. Systems Analysis (1950s and following)
    Cybernetic perspective (building control systems)
    Focus on dynamic interactions

5. Strategic Planning (1960s and 1970s)
    Diversification and search for synergies
    Redeployment of assets and restructuring

6. Japanese Management (1980s)
    Quality control systems involving people
    Novel approaches to inventory and production
    management

7. The Cognitive Perspective (1990s?)
    Emphasis on understanding how people think
    Recognition of errors made in managing information
    Use of artificial intelligence technology

In the 1950s, partially in reaction to the narrowness of some operations research, proponents of "systems analysis" started to look at organizations as wholes. In the 1960s and 1970s, "strategic planning" came into its own: first in the form of financial planning and forecasting, and then in the form of strategic management. Then in the 1980s increasing competition created the "Learn from Japan" movement, which ironically involved the recovery of management principles the United States had taught Japan prior to the ascendancy of the human relations and operations research movements.

All these movements still offer important lessons. But to advance further down the road toward excellence and competitive success, we need to better understand the most important processes of all: the processes of thinking. The cognitive perspective can help us do that.

Notes

The purpose of these chapter notes is to (1) to acknowledge the researchers whose work this book is based on, (2) to offer further commentary on technical or complex issues, and (3) to offer a guide to the relevant literature in case further information is desired. We hope readers will at least glance through these notes to appreciate the considerable scientific evidence on which this book rests.

Introduction: Decision-Making in the Real World

Page

xi–xii To fully acknowledge and cite the contributions of Daniel Kahneman and Amos Tversky are beyond the scope of this writing. However, a few central articles and books should be mentioned. Three papers by Kahneman and Tversky summarize their innovative work in quite accessible form: "Judgment Under Uncertainty: Heuristics and Biases," *Science* 185 (1974): 1124–31; "The Framing of Decisions and the Psychology of Choice," *Science* 211 (1981): 453–58; and "The Psychology of Preferences," *Scientific American*, January 1982, 160–73.

The work of Herbert Simon is even more widespread and difficult to acknowledge since it came earlier and influenced not only decision-making but much of cognitive science. However, a summary of his broad range of thinking on topics related to decision-making can be found in two books of invited lectures presented at MIT and Stanford respectively, *The Sciences of the Artificial*, 2d ed. (MIT Press, 1981) and *Reason in Human Affairs* (Stanford University Press, 1983). Also see his collected works in *Models of Man: Social and Rational* (John Wiley & Sons, 1957) and *Models of Discovery* (D. Reidel Publishing Co. Dordrecht, Holland, 1977).

xii The mathematical or decision analytic approach can be likened to building a "decision robot," in the form of a mathematical model. Once the "robot" is designed, to reflect a person's particular values and beliefs, it can substitute for this person in making trade-offs and

229

choices. However, if new situations arise, a human will still be necessary to judge if the robot is up to the task and if so to provide inputs. In Chapter 6, we examine further the pros and cons of substituting models for people.

xiii For readers who want to pursue the new approach to decision-making in more detail than our book allows, three excellent and highly readable books are available: *Judgment in Managerial Decision Making* by Max H. Bazerman (John Wiley & Sons, 1986); *Rational Choice in an Uncertain World* by Robyn M. Dawes (Harcourt Brace Jovanovich 1988), and *Judgment and Choice* by Robin Hogarth 2d ed. (John Wiley & Sons, 1987). The most influential of the primary literature has been reprinted in two anthologies, *Judgment Under Uncertainty: Heuristics and Biases*, edited by Daniel Kahneman, Paul Slovic, and Amos Tversky (Cambridge University Press, 1982) and *Judgment and Decision Making: An Interdisciplinary Reader*, edited by Hal R. Arkes and Kenneth R. Hammond (Cambridge University Press, 1986). A broader, integrative perspective is offered in *Decision Making: Descriptive, Normative and Prescriptive Interactions* edited by David Bell, Howard Raiffa, and Amos Tversky (Cambridge University Press, 1988).

xvi The ten traps described here reflect our personal views—based on consulting experiences and the research literature at large—as to the most common errors in decision-making in business. No such list, however, exists in the research literature per se, and it is doubtful that consensus could be reached on such a list among decision researchers.

Chapter 1: An Excellent Decision-Making Process

1 The continual breaking of athletic records is, of course, also in part due to improved equipment (e.g., vaulting poles or running shoes) as well as to increased numbers of people shooting for the record. The more people, over time, who attempt to break a record, the greater the sample becomes from which the record-breaker gets drawn. In many sports (e.g., swimming, speed skating, diving), however, the major factor in breaking records appears to be improved coaching and deeper insight into the physical and psychological aspects of the sport.

2 Thinking of decision-making as a process consisting of phases has a long intellectual tradition. John Dewey in Chapter 10 of his book

How We Think (D. C. Heath & Company, 1910) characterized problem-solving as consisting of (1) defining the problem, (2) identifying the alternatives, and (3) choosing the best one. Herbert Simon similarly proposed a three-phase process consisting of intelligence, design, and choice (see his *The New Science of Management* [Harper & Row, 1960]). Our four-phase framework especially highlights framing and learning (relative to other approaches).

5 There is little formal treatment of the concept of a metadecision in the research literature. However, several authors have discussed the problem of deciding how to decide. See, for instance, Eric J. Johnson and John W. Payne's article "Effort and Accuracy in Choice" (*Management Science*, 1985, vol. 30, pp. 395–414). Others have written wisely on the topic of decisions that might not get made (Ruth M. Corbin, "Decisions that Might Not Get Made," in *Cognitive Processes in Choice and Decision Behavior*, edited by Tom S. Wallsten [Lawrence Erlbaum, 1980]).

8 John Sculley's quotes were taken from pp. 20–22 in *Odyssey* by John Sculley (Harper & Row, 1987).

Chapter 2: The Power of Frames

15 The term "frame" originated in artificial intelligence research. Our concept of a decision frame is similar to Kahneman's and Tversky's, who define it as "the decision-maker's conception of the acts, outcomes, and contingencies associated with a particular choice" *Science* 211 [January 1981]: 453).

17 Why U.S. automakers bounded set-up time out of consideration in optimizing the manufacturing process is a fascinating question in its own right. (In the language of management science, changeover time was treated as a fixed parameter rather than a decision variable in the optimal production-inventory models.) Were there a few plant managers, engineers, or executives in the auto industry who saw beyond this boundary, but were unable to persuade others to work on reducing set-up times? Was the bounding out of these times encouraged by the separation between the developers of the optimization models, the operations researchers, and those directly responsible for production? We do not know the answers. However, we do know that it was not until the late 1970s that the problem was fully recognized and attacked by U.S. automakers. An analysis of Japanese auto production, with reference to interesting historical facts, can be found in "What Makes the Toyota Production System Really Tick" by Yasuhiro Monden (*Industrial Engineering* 13, no. 1 [January 1981]: 36–46).

18 The advertising example is based on an exercise conducted jointly with our colleague Harry Davis (Deputy Dean of the Graduate School of Business at the University of Chicago) in the context of a senior management program for the Interpublic Group of Companies. The participants were heads of local offices of such well-known agency systems as McCann-Erickson, SSC&B: Lintas, Campbell-Ewald, and others within the Interpublic Group of Companies.

21 The original ticket problem can be found in "The Framing of Decisions and the Psychology of Choice," by Amos Tversky and Daniel Kahneman (*Science* 211 [1981]: 457). It used a ticket price of ten dollars with college students asked to make the decision. When we first presented the ten-dollar version to managers, it made no difference whether the cash or ticket was lost because nearly everyone was willing to spend another ten dollars. We now use an "executive" price level of thirty or fifty dollars per ticket when we present this problem to professionals. At this price level, the demonstration seldom fails.

23 Functional blindness—i.e., the tendency to frame problems from one's own functional or occupational perspective—was demonstrated more systematically by DeWitt C. Dearborn and Herbert A. Simon in "Selective Perception: A Note on the Departmental Identification of Executives," *Sociometry* 21 (1958): 140–44.

24 The sunk-cost fallacy illustrates an improper drawing of mental boundaries. It occurs when costs that are truly sunk (i.e., incurred in the past) exert an influence on the current decision. Although it is a natural tendency to look back, this often interferes with sound decision-making. Many investors or traders, for instance, would be better off if they did not know the historical cost of their positions. As one investment pro (George Soros of Quantum Fund) put it, "I don't believe in making money back. Once you have lost, you have lost it. You lose it or make it, but you don't make it back" (*Fortune*, February 29, 1988, p. 113). For both academic and managerial analyses of sunk-cost fallacies see Richard Thaler, "Toward a Positive Theory of Consumer

NOTES

Choice," *Journal of Economic Behavior* 1 (1980): 50; Hal Arkes and Catherine Blumer, "The Psychology of Sunk Costs," *Organizational Behavior and Human Decision Processes* 35, no. 1 (1985): 124–40; and Barry M. Staw and Jerry Ross, "Knowing When to Pull the Plug," *Harvard Business Review* (March–April 1987). Thaler's article also discusses opportunity costs.

24 The marketing frame, also known in textbooks as the marketing concept, was popularized in a famous article titled "Marketing Myopia" by Theodore Levitt in the *Harvard Business Review* 38 (1960). It has become one of the most reprinted articles in the history of this leading business publication. The concept can be traced to earlier work by F. Jerome McCarthy (see Philip Kotler, *Marketing Management*, 5th ed. [Prentice-Hall, 1984]). The marketing frame has been crucial in defining the very idea of marketing, and in distinguishing it from a sales or production orientation.

It is currently argued, however, that the marketing frame needs revision. Aspects of the external environment previously bounded out of the marketing frame (viz., technology, politics and regulation, sociocultural factors) should be considered part of marketing managers' domain of action. For instance, success in international markets often requires the use of political power to lower import restrictions, hidden tariffs, and gatekeepers.

26 The experimental subjects in this study included 491 graduate students, 424 practicing physicians, and 238 ambulatory outpatients with chronic medical problems. We reported data on just a subset of the physicians. All three groups, however, fell victim to some kind of framing effects. Surgery was overall preferred to radiation therapy by 75 percent of those given the survival frame, but by only 58 percent of those given the mortality frame (see Barbara J. McNeil, Stephen G. Pauker, Harold C. Sox, and Amos Tversky in "On the Elicitation of Preferences for Alternative Therapies," *New England Journal of Medicine* 306, no. 21 [May 27, 1982]:1259–62). Anyone unsettled by this remarkable effect of framing in a life-and-death decision should appreciate that there is no single, correct frame. That is, neither the living nor dying reference point is necessarily more correct. As with so many problems in the real world, one frame presents a single view that is neither perfect nor complete. The best that decision-makers can strive

233

for is that the same decision is pointed to by more than one frame. When a different frame causes you to make a different decision, you have been warned that your decision is *frame-dependent*. You should then think more deeply about which frame better captures the problem you're facing.

The difference between living and dying typifies a large class of frame reversals, ranging from whether meat in a supermarket is considered 90 percent lean vs. 10 percent fat to whether closing an industrial plant entails saving or losing jobs. Below we present two versions for the plant-closing problem which typically result in opposite choices from managers depending on how we frame it.

Imagine that you are the regional head of a large labor union. One of your locals represents a manufacturing division belonging to a Fortune 500 company. Due to structural changes in the economy that are happening to union locals in other regions as well, this division's factories are threatened with a partial, and possibly complete, closure. They currently employ 600 members of your union.

The head of the manufacturing division and his staff have identified two options. The union's national consultants concur that these are the only two economically feasible alternatives for this division's factories. Both the head of the division and your national headquarters want to know which alternative you favor.

Option 1 entails a partial closure and the permanent dismissal of some workers. Option 2 entails taking a gamble that will end up with either zero or 600 jobs. Specifically the alternatives are as follows:

Version A

If option 1 is adopted exactly 200 jobs will be saved.
If option 2 is adopted there is a one-third chance that 600 jobs will be saved, and a two-thirds chance that no jobs will be saved.

Version B

If option 1 is adopted exactly 400 jobs will be lost.
If option 2 is adopted, there is a one-third chance that no jobs will be lost and a two-thirds chance that 600 jobs will be lost.

When we present these two different framings of the same problem to managers we typically find that a majority of managers favor option one, the conservative no-risk option, if we frame the decision in terms of jobs saved. However, a majority favor the other choice, the risky

234

uncertain alternative, when they are deciding the problem in the jobs-lost frame. This is a rather general phenomenon; people are more willing to accept risks in an attempt to escape losses, while preferring safety when faced with gains. Kahneman and Tversky formalized this tendency in a seminal article titled "Prospect Theory: An Analysis of Decision Under Risk," in *Econometrica* 47 (1979): 263–91. Much subsequent research has borne out the generality of this asymmetric attitude toward risk for gains vs. losses.

28 The discount example (concerning dollars vs. percentages) is originally due to Leonard J. Savage, *The Foundation of Statistics* (John Wiley & Son, 1954), p. 103 and Richard Thaler, "Toward a Positive Theory of Consumer Choice," *Journal of Economic Behavior and Organization* 1 (1980): 50. Although it is evident in this example that the correct yardstick is dollars rather than percentages, the choice of the proper yardstick can be quite unclear in more complex business situations. For example, should managers working for an American subsidiary in London formulate their local pricing decisions in dollars or pounds sterling? No simple answer exists here, as much depends on assumptions made about the efficiency of world capital markets. For a detailed treatment of thinking in local vs. headquarters currency see David J. Sharp, "Control Systems and Decision-Making in Multinational Firms: Price Management Under Floating Exchange Rates" (Ph. D. thesis, MIT, 1987), 298.

29 One footnote to the story of the Japanese airline pilot is that there were published but false reports that he later committed suicide. As we said, he was restricted to Asian routes and demoted to copilot, but he continued to fly with JAL.

29 The pervasive influence of metaphors is discussed in George Lakoff and Mark Johnson, *Metaphors We Live By* (University of Chicago Press, 1980). A more scholarly treatment concerning metaphors and categories of the mind in general is offered in George Lakoff's innovative and controversial book *Women, Fire and Dangerous Things* (University of Chicago Press, 1987).

30 The quotes from Ronald L. Singer concerning the launching of James River's paper products in the Northeast market are taken from "Manufacturer Establishes Beachhead in Paper War," *Marketing News*, December 7, 1984, p. 4.

32 For other examples of military frames in business see Al Ries and Jack Trout, *Marketing Warfare* (McGraw Hill, 1986), and David J. Rogers, *Waging Business Warfare* (Charles Scribner's Sons, 1987). Several of these popular books were anticipated by Philip Kotler and Ravi Singh's article, "Marketing Warfare in the 1980's," *The Journal of Business Strategy* 1, no. 3 (Winter 1981): 30–41.

33 What distinguishes thinking frames from decision frames is that the former are much more enduring and broadly used. Whereas a decision frame may be constructed for only one particular decision, a thinking frame represents a mental structure that has been built up over time and has become a permanent part of our mental repertoire. Our concept of a thinking frame is much closer to the original notion of frame as it appeared in the field of artificial intelligence in the mid-1970s. It was defined there as a method of organizing our knowledge about a concept to help focus attention and facilitate recall and inference. Thus, frames were defined as the mental structures or frameworks within which new information is interpreted through concepts acquired via previous experience. Our notion of thinking frames is also closely related to what are called schema and scripts in cognitive psychology. Like the artificial intelligence idea of a frame, schemas organize into a coherent whole a multitude of different component concepts and events.

34 The story of Darius the Persian king is taken from Herodotus, cited by Edward Beliaev, Thomas Mullen, and Betty Jane Punnett, "Understanding the Cultural Environment: U.S.-U.S.S.R. Trade Negotiations," in *California Management Review* (Winter 1985), pp. 100–12.

34 The family frame very much guides the thinking of Sam Johnson, the CEO of S. C. Johnson, Inc. See, for instance, the *New York Times* interview with Sam Johnson, "Managing When It's All in the Family," April 9, 1989, Business Section, p. 2. The details of Johnson's decision to fly over the entire British subsidiary can be found in a *Wall Street Journal* article, "Johnson's Gift to British Workers: An All Expenses Paid Trip to Racine" (1 October, 1984, p. 31).

Chapter 3: Winning Frames

38 The reframing of competitors is described in Michael E. Porter, *Competitive Strategy: Techniques for Analyzing Industries and Com-*

NOTES

petitors (Free Press, Macmillan Publishing Co., 1980). The five forces of competition identified there are suppliers, customers, rival firms, new entrants, and substitute products. Perhaps governments or regulators should be added as a sixth force.

39 Drucker, Peter. *Management: Task, Responsibilities, Practices.* (Harper & Row, 1974).

40 When Soichiro Honda introduced lightweight motorbikes into the United States in 1959, only 167 units were sold in the first year. In 1965, Honda sold 270,000 units. Although Honda is often cited as a case of brilliant Japanese strategy against a sleepy Harley-Davidson, we question that interpretation. Honda was neither well prepared, nor very strategic in its U.S. invasion. It succeeded, however, because it learned very quickly and listened to the market better than its competitors. For a critical discussion of conventional (mis)interpretations of the Honda story see Richard T. Pascale, "Perspectives on Strategy: The Real Story Behind Honda's Success," *California Management Review* (Spring 1984): 47–71.

46 For additional references (from simple to more complex) on creativity see Roger von Oech, *A Kick-in-the-Seat of the Pants* (Harper & Row, 1986); Edward de Bono, *Lateral Thinking* (Harper & Row, 1973); James Adams, *Conceptual Blockbusting* (Freeman, 1974); Chapter 8 in Robin Hogarth, *Judgment and Choice*, 2d ed. (John Wiley & Sons, 1987); or W. J. J. Gordon, *Synectics* (Harper & Row, 1961).

47 See Lee Iacocca's autobiography *Iacocca* (Bantam Books, 1984). Some of Vince Lombardi's advice is recounted on pp. 56–57.

47 The work of Robert Keidel can be found in his book *Game Plans: Sports Strategies for Business* (E. P. Dutton, 1985).

49 The original report, "Consumer Complaint Handling in America: Summary of Findings and Recommendations," from which the example of the complaining customers was taken was published by TARP, Inc. (September 1979).

51 The pollution example (of trapping vs. filtering) comes from Jordan D. Lewis, "Technology, Enterprise, and American Economic Growth," *Science* 215 (March 5, 1982):1204–11.

51 For excellent books on negotiation and framing see Roger Fisher and William Ury, *Getting to Yes: Negotiating Agreement Without Giving In* (Houghton Mifflin, 1981), or Howard Raiffa, *The Art and Science of Negotiation* (Harvard University Press, 1982).

52 For reframing in quality control see *Business Week*'s special report on quality, June 8, 1987, pp. 131–43. See also J. M. Juran, *Juran on Leadership for Quality* (Free Press, Macmillan Publishing Co., 1989).

54 The different modes for valuing a company are discussed in several places. A good reference is Brian H. Saffer's article, "Touching All Bases in Setting Merger Prices," *Mergers & Acquisitions* 19, no. 3 (Fall 1984): 42–48.

55 "The Parable of the Kitchen Spindle," by Elias H. Porter was published in the *Harvard Business Review* 40, no. 3 (May–June 1962): 58–66.

57 The use of scenarios at Royal Dutch/Shell (and strategic planning in general) is discussed by Pierre Wack in the *Harvard Business Review* (Fall 1985).

59 The Genentech example is discussed in more detail in *Fortune*, July 6, 1987, pp. 58–64. For 1988, the company declared a fourth-quarter loss of $15 million because of a $23 million charge against aging, unsold inventories of its heart drug tPA (*Wall Street Journal*, January 26, 1989, p. B5). Its stock dropped below twenty dollars a share (from a high of well over eighty dollars before the crash).

60 For an excellent discussion of opportunity-cost illusions see Richard Thaler, "Toward a Positive Theory of Consumer Choice," *Journal of Economic Behavior and Organization* 1 (1980): 39–60.

61–62 The four-square anecdote was recounted to us by a Chicago MBA student with permission from his friend Ken Carpenter.

Chapter 4: Knowing What You Don't Know

67 The remarkable life of Newton D. Baker is reported in *Newton D. Baker: A Biography* by C. H. Cramer (World Publishing Company, 1961). Baker's success in sending 2 million men to Europe in less than two years during World War I—in spite of the fact that he was a pacifist who, like President Wilson, initially opposed our entry into the war, was admired by John J. Pershing and Douglas MacArthur. Both of these commanders considered him the most able Secretary of War the country had ever known.

70 More systematic data on confidence ranges and probability calibration can be found in Sarah Lichtenstein, Baruch Fischhoff, and

Lawrence Phillips, "Calibration of Probabilities: The State of the Art to 1980," in *Judgment Under Uncertainty: Heuristics and Biases*, edited by Daniel Kahneman, Paul Slovic, and Amos Tversky (Cambridge University Press, 1982). This excellent overview also addresses the effects of feedback and training.

72 For a detailed overview of overconfidence studies see Sarah Lichtenstein, Baruch Fischhoff, and Lawrence Phillips, "Calibration of Probabilities: The State of the Art to 1980," in *Judgment Under Uncertainty: Heuristics and Biases* cited above. The data on physicians can be found in Jay J. Christensen-Szalanski and James B. Bushyhead, "Physician's Use of Probabilistic Information in a Real Clinical Setting," *Journal of Experimental Psychology: Human Perception and Performance* 7 (1981): 928–35. The data on physicists can be found in an unpublished paper by Max Henrion and Baruch Fischhoff, "Uncertainty Assessments in the Estimation of Physical Constants," (Carnegie-Mellon University, Department of Engineering and Public Policy, January 1984).

74 The overconfidence quotes are taken from *The Experts Speak* by Christopher Cerf and Victor Navasky (Pantheon Books, 1984). This excellent compendium contains thousands of authoritative misstatements from people in many walks of life.

75 Janis' book *Groupthink* (2d ed.) was published by Houghton Mifflin in 1981.

75 Ford's Edsel fiasco has been described many times. For a brief analysis see Robert F. Hartley, *Bullseyes and Blunders* (John Wiley & Sons, 1987).

75 The bias toward confirming evidence is discussed in Peter C. Wason, "On the Failure to Eliminate Hypotheses in a Conceptual Task," *Quarterly Journal of Experimental Psychology* 12 (1960): 129–40. A penetrating analysis of this complex issue has been presented by Joshua Klayman and Young-Won Ha, "Confirmation, Disconfirmation, and Information in Hypothesis Testing," *Psychological Review* 94, no. 2 (1987): 211–28. Klayman and Ha argue that whether disconfirmation or confirmation is most suitable depends in complex ways on the kind of task one faces.

76 The quotes are from James R. Emshoff and Ian I. Mitroff, "Improving the Effectiveness of Corporate Planning," *Business Horizons* 21 (1978): 49–60.

76 A discussion of the difference between primary and secondary knowledge can be found in the review article "Calibration of Probabilities," by Lichtenstein, Fischhoff, and Phillips cited above. The topic of secondary knowledge, or knowing what we know, is also related to what has come to be known as "metacognition." For example, see Ilan Yaniv and David E. Meyer, "Activation and Metacognition of Inaccessible Stored Information: Potential Bases for Incubation Effects in Problem Solving," *Journal of Experimental Psychology: Learning, Memory and Cognition* 13, no. 2 (1987): 187–205.

78 Stern's study is described in Thomas Spencer Jerome's essay "The Case of the Eyewitness: 'A Lie Is a Lie, Even in Latin,'" in *The Historian As Detective*, edited by R. W. Winks (Harper & Row, 1968). The original study was published in French in *L'Année Psychologique* XII (1906): 168–78.

78 The insignificant correlation between the confidence and accuracy of eyewitnesses is derived from work by Gary L. Wells and Donna M. Murray, "Eyewitness Confidence," in *Eyewitness Testimony: Psychological Perspectives*, edited by Gary L. Wells and Elizabeth F. Loftus (Cambridge University Press, 1984). Wells and Murray surveyed thirty-one studies and reported that the average correlation coefficient between accuracy and confidence was only .07. Since the publication of Wells and Murray's work other studies have been completed. Possibly the most optimistic of these (regarding the confidence-accuracy correlation) is work by Robert K. Bothwell, Kenneth A. Deffenbacher, and John C. Brigham, "Correlation of Eyewitness Accuracy and Confidence: Optimality Hypothesis Revisited," *Journal of Applied Psychology* 72, no. 4 (1987): 691–95. They examine studies in which events are staged so that eyewitnesses can be tested under controlled and often superior conditions. In this kind of situation the correlation between accuracy and confidence reaches .25. Their work is especially interesting because they focus on those factors that lead to a stronger relationship.

79 The distinction between deciders and doers reflects a rigid, hierarchical view of organizations with deciders at the top and doers at the bottom. In modern organizations decision responsibility is usually much more diffuse and closer to the time and place of action—i.e., the implementation of the decision. Among the first to articulate the modern view was Herbert Simon. The first page of his classic book *Administrative Behavior* (Macmillan: New York, 1957, 2d ed.; 1st ed., 1945) reads, in part: "Although any particular activity involves both 'deciding' and 'doing,' it has not commonly been realized that a theory of administration should be concerned with the process of decision as well as the process of action. . . . The task of 'deciding' pervades the entire administrative organization quite as much as does the task of 'doing'—indeed, it is integrally tied up with the latter."

81 The term "heuristic" has been used extensively in management science. These researchers often had to settle for approximate solutions (i.e., heuristic solutions) for problems that could not be solved optimally. There are many areas of human endeavor where heuristics play an important role. For example, playing chess can be viewed as developing an increasingly sophisticated series of heuristics (as one moves from novice to international grand master). A typical novice heuristic is "dominate the center squares." The heuristics of the masters are much more complex, reflecting their deeper knowledge of the game.

82–83 The data for the causes of death are taken from Barbara Combs and Paul Slovic, "Newspaper Coverage of Causes of Death," *Journalism Quarterly* 56 (1979): 837–43, 849. This striking demonstration has been replicated by others including foreign subjects. For example, see Connie M. Kristiansen, "Newspaper Coverage of Diseases and Actual Mortality Statistics," *European Journal of Social Psychology* 13 (1983): 193–94.

85 The IRS's use of availability around March and April is now so well known that newspapers have come to expect it. On March 8, 1982, the *Chicago Tribune* titled its article on the announcement of tax indictments "Annual Tax Warning: Twenty Indicted Here" (section 1, p. 17).

87 Florida was one of the pioneer states in the use of videotapes in courtroom evidence. The pros and cons of this technique are reviewed in detail in Rita Dee, "Videotape as a Tool in the Florida Legal Process," *Nova Law Journal* 5 (1981): 243–60.

87 The Concord Capital example is described in "Outpsyching the Market," *Forbes*, July 11, 1988. The president and founder, Harold Arbit, gave us the following additional background information on their hit product strategy and companies: "Worlds of Wonder went public in 1986, based on the success of the Teddy Ruxpin doll. At the time, it was

241

virtually a single-product company, although it did produce a second hit in 1987 (Laser Tag). When initially offered at above $20, the stock immediately rose to $29, giving it a market capitalization in excess of $700 million. This approached the market value of diversified industry leader Hasbro at $1 billion, and matched the *combined* value of the next 3 largest companies in the toy industry: Mattel ($300 million), Coleco ($200 million), and Kenner-Parker ($200 million). By mid-1988, Worlds of Wonder was bankrupt and its securities were worthless. Kenner-Parker was acquired for $600 million, Mattel and Hasbro had slight declines in their valuation levels, and Coleco was also sliding toward bankruptcy. Neither Mattel nor Hasbro has produced a hit since 1986. Our investment strategy was comprised of these two companies and Western Publishing. We purchased Western Publishing at $12 and sold it at $21 after they produced the hit product Pictionary. We still own Mattel (purchased at $8 and currently selling at $14) and Hasbro (purchased at $13 and currently selling at $18)." Personal communication, May 15, 1989.

88 The anchoring heuristic was first proposed by Paul Slovic and Sarah Lichtenstein in their paper "Comparison of Bayesian and Regression Approaches to the Study of Information Processing in Judgment," *Organizational Behavior and Human Performance* 6 (1971) 641–744, and further elaborated by Amos Tversky and Daniel Kahneman in "Judgment Under Uncertainty: Heuristics and Biases," *Science* 185 (1974): 1124–31.

89 The agents were asked to set a fair purchase price for a house. Each one was given a comprehensive packet of information, including a summary of all real estate sales in the neighborhood for the past six months. The information received by the agents described a real house that was actually for sale at a listing price of $74,000. However, the agents were never told this price. Instead, half were informed that the listing price was $65,900 (a low anchor), while the other half were given a high anchor of $83,900. They visited the house, considered as much information as they wished (except the true list price), and then decided on a fair purchase price for the house. The results: the low anchor group recommended an average price of $66,800, while the high anchor group thought $73,000 would be a fair price for the same house. We should remember that these agents knew they were being studied by researchers, so they were probably more careful than usual in judging the house's fair price. Still the estimates of the two groups were over $6000 apart (i.e., about 9% of the average appraised value). (See

Gregory B. Northcraft and Margaret A. Neale, "Experts, Amateurs, and Real Estate: An Anchoring-and-Adjustment Perspective on Property Pricing Decisions," *Organizational Behavior and Human Decision Processes* 39 [1987]:84–97).

90 The influence of even random anchors is described in Amos Tversky and Daniel Kahneman, "Judgment Under Uncertainty: Heuristics and Biases," *Science* 185 (1974): 1124–31. The above study with real estate agents showed that they were unable to ignore anchors when asked to.

92 A discussion of incrementalism can be found in the work of Charles E. Lindblom, "The Science of Muddling Through," *Public Administration Review* 19 (1959). See also Amitai Etzioni's article in *Public Administration Review* (December 1967): 385–92. The case for incrementalism, especially when dealing with strategic change, was made by James Brian Quinn in *Strategies for Change: Logical Incrementalism* (Richard D. Irwin, 1980). The arguments against it are discussed in Irving L. Janis, *Crucial Decisions: Leadership in Policymaking and Crisis Management*, The Free Press, Macmillan, New York, 1989.

Chapter 5: Improving Your Intelligence-Gathering

96 To be exact, the probability of missing an 80 percent confidence range three times in a row is $(.2)^3$ or less than 1 percent (assuming statistical independence among the forecasts). Thus we can be pretty sure in this case that the sales manager is overconfident and poorly calibrated.

Another possibility is that the manager deliberately biases the estimates, because of the way incentives are structured. For example, most real-estate agents have a bias to overestimate the value of your house, so as to get the listing. And if you asked them for a confidence range, they may purposely give you a narrow range (to offer positive assurance). In such cases, more sophisticated procedures may be called for to counter the bias. For example, the agent could be told that 7 percent commission will be received if the house listed at $150,000 sells within $10,000 of the list price, 6 percent if within $20,000, etc. This will reduce (upward) biases in the point estimates. Similarly you could offer a higher commission if the house sells within the agent's confidence range than when it falls outside. This would provide a counterbalance to the agent's natural and strategic bias to provide narrow ranges.

An extensive academic literature exists addressing this problem in quantitative form. The principal-agent literature (see Steve Ross, "The Economic Theory of Agency: The Principal's Problem," *American Economic Review*, 1973, 63, 134–39 or Michael Jensen and William H. Meckling, "Theory of the Firm: Managerial Behavior, Agency Costs, and Ownership Structure," *Journal of Financial Economics*, 1976, 3, 305–60) addresses how to set incentives (in firms) so that agents do in fact act in the best interest of the principal (who is usually less well informed and may have a different utility function). The so-called scoring rule literature (James E. Matheson and Robert Winkler, "Scoring Rules for Continuous Probability Distributions," *Management Science*, 1976, 22, 1087–96) examines how to extract from someone honest judgments by providing incentive (or scoring) rules that make truthful disclosure the optimal strategy.

100   The excellent calibration of weather forecasters is documented in Allan Murphy and Robert Winkler, "Probability Forecasting in Meteorology" *Journal of the American Statistical Association* (September 1984). For bridge players see Gideon Keren, "Facing Uncertainty in the Game of Bridge: A Calibration Study," in *Organizational Behavior and Human Decision Processes*, vol. 39, 1987, pp. 98–114. For accountants, see Lawrence A. Tomassini, Ira Solomon, Marshall B. Romney, Jack L. Krogstad, "Calibration of Auditors' Probabilistic Judgments: Some Empirical Evidence," in *Organizational Behavior and Human Performance*, vol. 30, 1982, pp. 391–406.

100   George Moore's book *The Banker's Life* was published by W. W. Norton & Co. in 1987.

104   The breaking of the German code is described in Andrew Hodges' excellent biography *Alan Turing: The Enigma* (Simon & Schuster, 1984).

106   Xerox's attempt to anticipate problems in the early stages of the design process is described in Robert C. Wood, "Quality by Design," *The Quality Review* (Spring 1988): 22–27.

107   The study of restaurant managers can be found in Laurette Dube-Rioux and J. Edward Russo, "An Availability Bias in Professional Judgment," (*Journal of Behavioral Decision Making* 1, 1988: 223–37).

109   For further discussion of the scenario approach to planning and decision-making, see two articles by Pierre Wack, "Scenarios: Un-

244

charted Waters Ahead," *Harvard Business Review* (September–October 1985): 73–89, and "Scenarios: Shooting the Rapids," *Harvard Business Review* (November–December 1985): 139–50; William R. Huss, "A Move Toward Scenarios," *International Journal of Forecasting*, 4 (1988): 377–88; Paul J. H. Schoemaker, "Scenario Thinking" (Working paper, Center for Decision Research, University of Chicago, 1989).

112 The idea of prospective hindsight is discussed and documented in Deborah J. Mitchell, J. Edward Russo, and Nancy Pennington, "Back to the Future: Temporal Perspective in the Explanation of Events," (*Journal of Behavioral Decision Making* 2, 1989: 25–39).

113 The data for the horse-race handicappers are from an unpublished study by Paul Slovic and Bernard Corrigan (formerly at the Oregon Research Institute). The essentially flat curve for accuracy results from three of the eight handicappers decreasing in accuracy, two improving, and three staying about the same. In an unpublished paper prepared for a seminar titled "Behavioral Problems of Adhering to a Decision Policy," Slovic attributes the flat curve to information overload. For example, when the handicappers were presented with the same races a second time (to test their consistency) they proved less consistent with forty pieces of information than with five or ten. We gratefully acknowledge Paul Slovic for providing us with the necessary background information on this telling study.

114 The reasons why experienced decision-makers processing large amounts of information do not extract the maximum benefit are not well understood. We believe that they are often distracted by unusual values (such as extreme cases). Also, there is a tendency to be unduly influenced by the first and last data items seen and to give less weight to those in the middle. Although experts are often good at "chunking" large amounts of data into easily remembered portions or subtotals, they still fall victim to information overload. A remarkable series of articles by Lynne Reder of Carnegie-Mellon University contrasted a 1,000-word summary with the original 5,000-word introductory chapter in a college textbook (on African geography). She and her coauthors found that students, when given equal time (twenty to thirty minutes), learned more from the summary. Based on quizzes using objective questions, the summary proved superior to the full text in (1) remembering explicitly stated information, (2) inferring information implied but not

245

DECISION TRAPS

explicitly stated over periods as long as twelve months, and (3) learning new information (e.g., additional insight into African geography).

Chapter 6: Making the Choice

119 There exist many different meanings and views on the role of intuition. For some, intuitive decision-making denotes the height of human intellectual achievement, whereas others view it as a self-serving cover for ignorance. Our view of intuition lies toward the positive side. We believe intuition is based on accumulated experience and concerns the quick apprehension or understanding of a situation without conscious analytical thought. Intuition might be described as tacit knowledge. This view of intuition is quite close to that of Herbert A. Simon, as recently stated in an article jointly written with Michael J. Prietula, "The Experts in Your Midst," *Harvard Business Review*, (January–February 1989): 120–124. Other articles of interest on the role of intuition include one by Hillel J. Einhorn, "Accepting Error to Make Less Error" *Journal of Personality Assessment* 50 no. 3 (1986): 387–95; and Kenneth R. Hammond, Robert M. Hamm, Janet Grassia, and Tamra Pearson, "Direct Comparison of the Efficacy of Intuitive and Analytical Cognition in Expert Judgment," *IEEE Transactions on Systems, Man, and Cybernetics* SMC-17, no. 5 (September–October 1987).

120 Taking less time and effort to make a decision is an important consideration that decision research increasingly appreciates. Making the best decision means not only choosing the best alternative (referred to as maximizing the utility of the chosen alternative), but also minimizing time, effort and other decision-making costs. This perspective is discussed in J. Edward Russo and Barbara A. Dosher, "Strategies for Multiattribute Binary Choise," *Journal of Experiemental Psychology: Learning, Memory and Cognition*, 9 (1983): 676–96, and in Eric J. Johnson and John W. Payne, "Effort and Accuracy in Choice," *Management Science*, 30 (1985): 395–414.

121 The radiologist example was taken from Paul J. Hoffman, Paul Slovic, and L. G. Rorer, "An Analysis-of-Variance Model for Assessment of Configural Cue Utilization in Clinical Judgment," *Psychological Bulletin* 69 (1968): 338–49.

122 The tonsillectomy data came from H. Baskin, *New England*

NOTES

Journal of Medicine (1945): 232–691. See also *Physical Defects: The Pathway to Correction*, New York: American Child Health Associa tion, 1934.

122 Although two of our examples regarding human inconsistency entail medical judgments, we do not wish to suggest that doctors are somehow worse than other professionals when it comes to judgment or choice. Indeed, the medical profession is one of the few that has founded a Society for Medical Decision Making, with its own scholarly journal (*Medical Decision Making*). We know of no other such society for legal, architectural, engineering or other professional specialties. Medicine has the additional benefit— from a research viewpoint—that the actual outcomes are often obtainable (e.g., via autopsies). In contrast, with legal predictions (on, say, guilt or innocence) the truth may never be known for sure.

125 The story of the food products company and its scientific rule is quite troubling. The junior manager who heard us lecture on the topic recognized the problem and explained it to his superiors. They were either unable to understand the trap they had fallen into or unwilling to hear the message. The company did not correct the problem, and the junior manager eventually left the firm. In fairness to his superiors, the problem is quite subtle. We discuss here in detail what seems to have happened to illustrate (1) how intricate some of these biases are and (2), how carefully some of the underlying heuristics have been analyzed in the research literature.

The company narrowed the decision between the old-fashioned and cost-reduced versions of the new product down to two considerations; consumer acceptance and cost. Following standard consumer marketing principles they next decided that consumer acceptance was more important than cost. (One reason for emphasizing product quality over cost was that the brand managers in this company were rewarded for short-term profits. Since they managed a brand for only eighteen to twenty-four months, managers were strongly tempted to cut both quality and cost. The cost saving would show up immediately while the lowered quality would impact sales slowly. This would give them an outstanding bottom line and the prospect of promotion and increased responsibility, while leaving the next brand manager holding the bag with respect to lowered market share.)

Of course, measuring consumer acceptance is not as simple as measuring height. It can't be done that precisely. However, careful market research techniques can be used, including comparative taste tests of the old-fashioned and cost-reduced versions. Nonetheless, even after several hundred people have tasted your product and given their judgments, there is still some uncertainty about which brand is better (especially if taste quality is very close). For this reason the firm used a standard marketing research protocol and a test of statistical significance to determine whether the cost-reduced version was reliably lower in taste quality than the old-fashioned version.

Unfortunately, all this sophistication may lead to a circularity trap. Here's how it works. Imagine three cookies, A, B, and C, and their ratings on taste quality (using a 0–20 scale) and cost (on a 0–100 scale) as shown below.

Cookies	Taste Quality	Cost of Formulation
A	15	39
B	14	36
C	13	34

The decision heuristic that the company used is equivalent to saying the following. "I will always choose whichever brand is higher in taste quality (and completely ignore cost advantages) except when two brands are tied or almost tied on quality. Then I will turn to cost as the determining factor." To determine whether two cookies were "almost tied" on taste quality the company used a test of statistical significance.

So, what happens when cookies A and B are compared? Let's say that a difference of one rating point in taste quality is not statistically significant. This means that cookies A and B are tied on taste quality and hence we turn to cost, causing B to be selected. When we compare cookies B and C, the same logic leads to the choice of C. Now here's the trap. When we compare A and C, the difference in taste quality is now *two* units, which is a statistically significant difference, so we cannot choose the cost-reduced version C but must choose A over C. However, this implies a disturbing circularity of preferences. We cannot consistently prefer B over A, C over B, but A over C. That this is illogical is easily shown by turning anyone who holds those preferences into a "money pump." It would be done as follows.

248

Assume that some party truly prefers B to A, C to B, and A to C. Assuming you own B and C and they own A, then the following can happen. They prefer B to A and hence there must be some amount of money that they would be willing to pay you to obtain B (in exchange for A). Suppose you make the trade, so they now have B and you have A and C plus, say, one dollar. But now they would prefer C to B, so again you trade, taking B plus one dollar from them and giving C in return. Now you have A and B and two dollars of their money while they have C. The circularity is completed when you offer them A for C and one dollar. You end up with B and C while they end up with A just where you both started. The only difference is that you also have three dollars of their money. As long as they maintain this circularity of preferences, you can keep pumping three dollars out of them every time you go around the circle.

When we present this circularity to managers many of them think it is awkward, even embarrassing, but not necessarily dangerous. However, it is exactly this circularity trap that the major food products company fell into. They kept picking B over A and then C over B, and, actually, D over C and E over D until they had significantly undermined their market share and their profits. They could have easily seen this if only they had compared C with A, as consumers implicitly did when comparing C with unchanged competitor brands.

For a highly technical review of the circularity trap see Peter C. Fishburn, "Lexicographic Orders, Utilities and Decision Rules: A Survey," *Management Science* (July 1974): 1442–71, as well as Amos Tversky's original analysis, "Intransitivity of Preferences," *Psychological Review*, 1969, 76, pp. 31–48.

125 For further analysis of screening rules see Hillel J. Einhorn, "The Use of Nonlinear, Noncompensatory Models in Decision Making," *Psychological Bulletin* 81 (1974): 97–106 and "Use of Nonlinear, Noncompensatory Models as a Function of Task and Amount of Information," *Organizational Behavior and Human Performance* 6 (1971): 1–27. See also Amos Tversky, "Elimination by Aspects: A Theory of Choice," *Psychological Review* 79 (1972): 281–99.

126 We would have liked to report a happy ending to the company story but cannot. The firm's senior management eventually realized that something was wrong with their products and ordered a "from scratch" reformulation. This process produced competitive products again, but at a high cost. And because the firm continued to use the faulty decision rule, it remained exposed to another gradual and to them mysterious decline of market share.

The message here is that most decision heuristics, even ones that seem very scientific, have built-in dangers. Those not aware of the nature of their heuristics and the kinds of dangers they pose will sooner or later pay the price of ignorance. In fairness to the managers involved, the decision trap here is one of the subtlest we have seen.

126 The Procter & Gamble heuristic, the Trammell Crow example, as well as the box on page 127, were all taken from Seth Gordin and Chip Conley, *Business Rules of Thumb* (Warner Books, 1987).

126 The topic of pricing is both important and complex. Interested readers might wish to consult Tom Nagle, *The Strategy and Tactics of Pricing* (Prentice-Hall, 1987) or Timothy M. Devinney, *Issues in Pricing: Theory and Research*, (Lexington Books, D. C. Heath and Company, 1988).

127 The letter by Ben Franklin on page 129 was sent in 1772 to Joseph Priestley (the famed British scientist and codiscoverer of oxygen). It has been reprinted in *The Benjamin Franklin Sampler* (Fawcett, 1956) as well as in several books on multiattribute decision-making (e.g., Milan Zeleny's *Multiple Criteria Decision Making* [McGraw-Hill Book Company]). Franklin's letter is one of the first systematic attempts to make subjective trade-offs explicit.

131 The linear model has a history of well over fifty years. A seminal work was Paul Meehl's *Clinical Versus Statistical Prediction* (University of Minnesota Press, 1954). A primary contributor to the subsequent work is Robyn Dawes of Carnegie-Mellon University. Two of his papers are particularly accessible to nonprofessional readers: "Clinical Versus Actuarial Judgment" written jointly with David Faust and Paul Meehl, *Science* 243 (1989): 1668–73, and "The Robust Beauty of Improper Linear Models in Decision Making," *American Psychologist* 34 (1979): 571–82. The 1979 Dawes paper is also reprinted in the anthology *Judgment Under Uncertainty: Heuristics and Biases*, edited by Daniel Kahneman, Paul Slovic, and Amos Tversky (Cambridge University Press, 1982).

135 The use of bootstrapping was systematically examined by Lewis R. Goldberg, "Man Versus Model of Man: A Rationale, Plus

Some Evidence for a Method of Improving on Clinical Inferences," *Psychological Bulletin* 73 (1970): 422–32 and Robyn M. Dawes, and Bernard Corrigan, "Linear Models in Decision Making," *Psychological Bulletin* 81 (1974): 87–106.

137 Table 2 was taken from Colin Camerer, "General Conditions for the Success of Bootstrapping Models," *Organizational Behavior and Human Performance* 27 (1981): 411–22. Striking evidence for the power of linear models is provided by Robyn M. Dawes and Bernard Corrigan, "Linear Models in Decision Making," *Psychological Bulletin* 81 (1974): 97–106, showing that the exact weights you use don't make much difference. They show that little predictive accuracy is lost changing from optimal to equal to random (!) weights. The all-important conclusion is that humans should find more and better predictors, but let models combine this information in a consistent fashion. See also Hillel J. Einhorn and Robin M. Hogarth, "Unit Weighting Schemes for Decision Making," *Organizational Behavior and Human Performance* 13 (1975): 171–92 or Howard Wainer, "Estimating Coefficients in Linear Models: It Don't Make No Nevermind," *Psychological Bulletin* 83 (1976): 213–17.

140 The credit-scoring table used by a national retailer was taken from Noel Capon, "Credit Scoring Systems: A Critical Analysis," *Journal of Marketing* 46 (1982): 82–91.

142 Alternative methods for obtaining weights in subjective linear models are discussed and empirically compared in Paul J. H. Schoemaker and Carter C. Waid, "An Experimental Comparison of Different Approaches to Determining Weights in Additive Utility Models," *Management Science* 28, no. 2 (1982): 182–96.

142 The multiattribute utility model is discussed in George P. Huber, "Multi-attribute Utility Models: A Review of Field and Field-Like Studies," *Management Science* 20 (1974): 1391–1402 and Ralph L. Keeney, and Howard Raiffa, *Decisions with Multiple Objectives*, John Wiley & Sons, 1976.

142 There is one alternative to using intuition or simple decision rules for less important decisions (where only a little effort can be justified). Change the decision environment so that less effort can still produce a good decision. This strategy has succeeded for ordinary consumer decisions where great effort is seldom justified. Creating an easier decision environment has worked for mortgage rates, unit prices, energy consumption, and the sugar content of food. See J. Edward Russo, "Information Processing from the Consumer's Perspective," in E. Scott Maynes (ed.), *The Frontier of Research in the Consumer Interest, Columbia, Missouri: American Council on Consumer Interests*, 1988.

142 The trade-offs involved in using various decision rules are discussed and empirically examined in John W. Payne, "Task Complexity and Contingent Processing in Decision Making: An Information Search and Protocol Analysis," *Organizational Behavior and Human Performance* 16 (1976): 366–87.

143 The formal or quantitative approach to decision-making is well explained in Howard Raiffa's *Decision Analysis: Introductory Lectures on Choices Under Uncertainty* (Addison-Wesley, 1968) and at a more advanced level in Ralph Keeney and Howard Raiffa, *Decisions with Multiple Objectives: Preferences and Value Tradeoffs* (John Wiley & Sons, 1976). For behaviorally oriented perspectives, see Detlof von Winterfeldt and Ward Edwards, *Decision Analysis and Behavioral Research* (Cambridge University Press, 1986) or Paul J. H. Schoemaker, "The Expected Utility Model: Its Variants, Purposes, Evidence and Limitations," *Journal of Economic Literature* 20 (June 1982): 529–63.

The basic idea underlying normative decision theory is to identify clearly one's options and objectives, and then to model quantitatively the possible outcomes and their probabilities. In addition, the decision-maker's values (or utilities) for various outcomes would need to be modeled so that a mathematical formula can be applied. The operationality of this approach, however, has been called into question due to the kind of biases discussed in this book; see John C. Hershey, Howard C. Kunreuther and Paul J. H. Schoemaker, "Sources of Bias in Assessment Procedures for Utility Functions," *Management Science*, 28, 8 (1982): 936–54.

Normative decision theory seeks to construct a decision robot (i.e., a formal model) that can replace decision-makers once their beliefs and values (i.e., goals, utilities, and risk-attitudes) have been measured. Our approach tries to aid the decision-maker by pointing out common decision traps and providing selective guidance on how to proceed. This, we believe, permits more creative and fluid decision-making.

The formal approach to decision-making goes back at least as far as

NOTES

Daniel Bernoulli's 1738 analysis of decision-making under risk (see L. Sommer's translation from Latin in *Econometrica* 22 [1954]: 23–36) and even earlier attempts to formalize the role of probability in games of chance (see Ian Hacking, *The Emergency of Probability* [Cambridge University Press, 1975]).

Chapter 7: Group Decisions

146 Kennedy's quote and further analysis of the Bay of Pigs fiasco are provided in Irving Janis, *Groupthink* (2d ed.) (Houghton Mifflin, 1982). For a shorter analysis see Irving L. Janis, "Groupthink," *Psychology Today*, November 1971, pp. 43–46, 74–76.

147 General Motors' Corvair problems are discussed in J. Patrick Wright, *On a Clear Day You Can See General Motors* (Wright Enterprises, 1979) and Ed Cray, *Chrome Colossus: General Motors and Its Times* (McGraw-Hill, 1980).

147 The space shuttle disaster is examined in "Report of the Presidential Commission on the Space Shuttle Challenger Accident," I and II (June 6, 1986). Also see the SCRHAAC Report, *Post-Challenger Evaluation of Space Shuttle Risk Assessment and Management* (National Academic Press, 1988). For the link to groupthink, see James K. Esser and Joanne S. Lindoerfer. "Group-Think and the Space Shuttle *Challenger* Accident: Toward a Quantitative Case Analysis," *Journal of Behavioral Decision Making*, 2 (3) (1989): 167–78.

150 Asch's classic conformity experiment was first published in Solomon E. Asch, "Studies of Independence and Submission to Group Pressure," *Psychological Monograms* 70 (1956). Subsequent extensions are reviewed in Serge Moscovici, "Social Influence and Conformity," in *The Handbook of Social Psychology*, edited by Gardner Lindzey and Elliot Aronson, 3d ed. (Random House, 1985). See also, Vernon L. Allen and John M. Levine, "Social Support, Dissent, and Conformity," *Sociometry* 31 (1968): 138–49.

153 The three profiles of group decisions in Fig. 3 were suggested to us by John Carroll of MIT during some of our joint seminars. We gratefully acknowledge his contribution.

155 Unlike the individual decision literature, the research on group decision making does not allow for easy generalizations. Much depends on context, group size, distribution of power, cohesion, task complexity, role of the leader, deadlines, differences in status, etc. Thus, our focus on cohesion and order of prior opinion as two key factors in predicting group shifts is only part (although a very important part) of a complex picture.

156 The Myers-Briggs test of cognitive style is discussed in Isabel Briggs Myers and Mary H. McCaulley, *Manual: A Guide to the Development and Use of the Myers-Briggs Type Indicator* (Consulting Psychologists Press, 1985). The test is based on Carl Jung's book *Psychological Types* (Harcourt Brace, 1923). See also Isabel Briggs Myers, *Gifts Differing* (Consulting Psychologists Press, 1988).

156 The Harold Geneen and Robert McNamara examples of differences in cognitive style were taken from Alan Rowe and Richard Mason, *Managing with Style: A Guide to Understanding, Assessing and Improving Decision Making* (Jossey-Bass, 1987).

157 The decision characteristics in the box on page 158 were adapted from James L. McKenney and Peter Keen, "How Managers' Minds Work," *Harvard Business Review* (May–June 1974): 79–90.

162–165 The Denver Police Department controversy and its resolution are explained in Kenneth R. Hammond, and Leonard Adelman, "Science, Values and Human Judgment," *Science* (1976): 389–96. Also see Kenneth R. Hammond, et al., "Linking Environmental Models with Models of Human Judgment: A Symmetrical Decision Aid," *Transactions on Systems, Man and Cybernetics* (1977) SMC-7.

166 The general notion of separating values from facts is further examined in Peter C. Gardiner and Ward Edwards, "Public Values: Multiattribute Utility Measurement for Social Decision Making," in *Human Judgment and Decision Processes*, edited by Martin F. Kaplan and Steven Schwartz (Academic Press, 1975).

Chapter 8: Why People Fail to Learn

173 The Christmas drawing of the Spanish lottery is called *El Gordo*. In 1988 this prize amounted to $159 million, which is still the largest lottery prize in the world in spite of the recent megaprizes in U.S. state lotteries. The story of the winner who did not know that 7 × 7 = 49 is retold in a *Los Angeles Times* article of Friday, December 30, 1977, pt. 1, p. 13.

175 The results of the Bender Gestalt experiments are published in an article by Lewis R. Goldberg, "The Effectiveness of Clinicians' Judgments: The Diagnosis of Organic Brain Damage from the Bender Gestalt Test," *Journal of Consulting Psychology* 23 (1959): 25–33. It is important to emphasize that learning to use this test well is possible: the expert showed that. The point is that average clinicians using this test failed to learn *automatically* from experience. Learning often requires a focus on learning itself.

177 The need to feel in control is discussed more fully in Ellen Langer, "The Illusion of Control," *Journal of Personality and Social Psychology* 32 (1975): 311–28. The examples involving dental patients and workers in noisy circumstances are discussed in Lawrence C. Perlmuter and Richard A. Monty, "The Importance of Perceived Control: Fact or Fantasy?" *American Scientist* 65 (November-December 1977): 759–65. Shelley E. Taylor and Jonathon D. Brown offer an interesting perspective on the positive value of illusions in "Illusion and Well-Being: A Social Psychological Perspective on Mental Health," *Psychological Bulletin*, 193, no. 2 (1988): 193–210.

178 The illusion of control exhibited by the management of the Indiana Pacers concerning the 1983 National Basketball Association player draft is described in the May 19, 1983, edition of the Palatine, Illinois, *Daily Herald*, sec. 4, p. 2.

179 A pointed discussion of the subtle ways in which we rationalize is offered by Elliot Aronson's article "The Rationalizing Animal," *Psychology Today*, 1973.

180 The Rand report data were taken from "Understanding Cost Growth and Performance Shortfalls in Pioneer Process Plants," by Edward W. Merrow, Kenneth E. Phillips, and Christopher W. Myers, September 1981, Rand Corporation Report R-2569-DOE, prepared for the U.S. Department of Energy, and "A Review of Cost Estimation in New Technologies: Implications for Energy Process Plants," by Edward W. Merrow, Stephen W. Chapel, and Christopher Worthy, July 1979, Rand Corporation Report R-2481-DOE, also prepared for the Department of Energy.

180–181 The self-serving attribution bias of CEOs' letters to shareholders can be found in work by Gerald Salancik and James Meindl "Corporate Attributions as Strategic Illusions of Management Control," *Administrative Science Quarterly* 29 (1984): 238–54.

183 The hindsight bias and the story of Nixon's trips to China can be found in an article by Baruch Fischhoff and Ruth Beyth titled "'I Knew It Would Happen'—Remembered Probabilities of Once-Future Things," *Organizational Behavior and Human Performance* 13 (1975): 1–16. The hindsight bias is especially problematic in legal trials, where witnesses' memories get distorted. The accuracy and confidence of eyewitness testimony are discussed in *Eyewitness Testimony: Psychological Perspectives,* edited by Gary L. Wells and Elizabeth F. Loftus (Cambridge University Press, 1984). See also Eugene Winograd's review "What You Should Know About Eyewitness Testimony" in *Contemporary Psychology* 31, no. 5 (1986): 332–34.

187 A fuller discussion of self-serving attribution biases can be found in Richard Nisbett and Lee Ross, *Human Inference: Strategies and Shortcomings of Social Judgments* (Prentice-Hall, 1980).

Chapter 9: Improving Feedback

190 The problems of missing feedback and treatment effects are discussed by Hillel J. Einhorn in his chapter "Learning from Experience and Suboptimal Rules in Decision Making," in *Cognitive Processes in Choice and Decision Behavior,* edited by Thomas S. Wallsten (Lawrence Erlbaum, 1980). A more detailed analysis can be found in Hillel J. Einhorn and Robin M. Hogarth, "Confidence in Judgment: Persistence of the Illusion of Validity," *Psychological Review* 85 (1978): 395–416.

190–91 One industry, money management, is becoming increasingly interested in tracking—via shadow portfolios—the normally missing cells. Once analysts have made their stock recommendations, policy committees typically decide how much money to invest in each. However, the more sophisticated of these firms also analyze how well the recommendations they *rejected* would have done. Because feedback (in the form of market prices) is available for both the accepted and rejected stocks, management can compare the quality of different analysts' recommendations without having to buy the stocks themselves. Indeed, in some firms we know (e.g., Concord Capital), analysts' annual compensation is based on the performance of their complete "shadow portfolios"—all the stocks that they recommended, not just the ones they convinced the policy committee to invest in.

NOTES

192 The predictions from *Bartender* magazine are summarized in the July 12, 1982, issue of the *Chicago Tribune*, sec. 3, p. 2.

193 The study on "late bloomers" was conducted by Robert Rosenthal and Lenore Jacobson and published in their book *Pygmalion in the Classroom* (Holt Rinehart & Winston, 1968). A review of how exactly the self-fulfilling prophecy about students' performance takes place has been offered by Lee Jussim, "Self-Fulfilling Prophecies: A Theoretical and Integrative Review," *Psychological Review* 93, no. 4 (1986): 429–45. See also Robert K. Merton, "The Self-fulfilling Prophecy," in his book *Social Theory and Social Structure* (Macmillan Publishing Co., 1968).

194 The self-fulfilling prophecy also shows up in job interviews. Noteworthy here is the work of Robert Dipboye, "Self-Fulfilling Prophecies in the Selection-Recruitment Interview," *Academy of Management Review* 7 (1982): 579–86. This classic study has been replicated and analyzed thoroughly. An analysis of the larger issues of the impact of expectancies on actual behavior was written by Edward E. Jones, "Interpreting Interpersonal Behavior: The Effects of Expectancies," *Science* 234, no. 3 (October 1986): 41–46). See also David H. Tucker, and Patricia M. Rowe, "Relationship Between Expectancy, Causal Attributions, and Final Hiring Decisions in the Employment Interview," *Journal of Applied Psychology* 64 (1979): 27–34.

195 Our inability to detect relationships between variables when masked by noise is discussed further in Dennis L. Jennings, Teresa M. Amabile, and Lee Ross, "Informal Covariation Assessment: Data-Based Versus Theory-Based Judgments," in *Judgment Under Uncertainty: Heuristics and Biases*, edited by Daniel Kahneman, Paul Slovic, and Amos Tversky (Cambridge University Press, 1982).

197–98 The space shuttle examples (Figures 6 and 7) were taken from Siddhartha R. Dalal, Edward B. Fowlkes, and Bruce Hoadley, "Risk Analysis of the Space Shuttle: Pre-*Challenger* Prediction of Failure" (*Journal of the American Statistical Association*, December 1989, Vol. 84, No. 408, pp. 945–957.)

203 The remarkable study by the Bell System is reported by J. L. Showers and L. M. Chakrin in their paper, "Reducing Uncollectible Revenues from Residential Telephone Customers," *Interfaces* 11 (1981): 21–31.

204 For more on David Ogilvy's approach to advertising see his autobiography *Ogilvy on Advertising* (Vintage Books, 1985) or his earlier book *Confessions of an Advertising Man* (Ballantine Books, 1963).

Chapter 10: Changing Your Way of Deciding

215 For additional examples of decision audits, see E. Frank Harrison, *The Managerial Decision-Making Process* (Houghton Mifflin, 1981) concerning the Cuban Missile Crises and the TFX bomber plane (i.e., Robert McNamara's failed attempt to have the U.S. Navy and Air Force *jointly* develop a sophisticated fighter plane circa 1962). Brief audits of five bad decisions are offered in Paul C. Nutt's *Making Tough Decisions* (Jossey-Bass Publishers, 1989) involving (1) President Carter's failed Iranian rescue mission, (2) RCA's $175 million video disc fiasco, (3) San Francisco's embarrassing Bay Area Rapid Transit (BART) system, (4) record cost overruns in building a stunning Opera House in Sydney, Australia, and (5) ITT's ill-fated construction of a pulp paper plant that had to be closed within five years.

Regarding the Cuban Missile Crisis, also see Graham Allison's classic *The Essence of Decision*, Prentice-Hall, 1967. For direct contrasts between good and bad decisions involving the same industries see Robert Hartley's *Bullseyes and Blunders*, John C. Wiley, New York, 1987. An interesting analysis of "Great Japanese Mistakes" is offered in *Fortune* (February 13, 1989): 108–11.

220 For a summary of British Petroleum's decision auditing see F. Gulliver, "Post-project Appraisals Pay," *Harvard Business Review* (March–April 1987): 128–32.

Epilogue: Thinking About Thinking: The Key to Managing in the 1990s?

225 For further nontechnical detail on the development of cognitive science see Morton Hunt, *The Universe Within: A New Science Explores the Human Mind* (Simon & Schuster, 1982) or Howard Gardner, *The Mind's New Science: A History of the Cognitive Revolution* (Basic Books, 1985).

225–28 The early history of management ideas is reviewed in Harwood F. Merrill, *Classics in Management* (American Management Association, 1970).

For an introduction to the systems view of management, see Stafford Beer, *The Brain of the Firm*, John Wilcy and Sons, 1981 (first edition, 1972, the Penguin Press).

The Japanese are very much betting on the cognitive approach via their ambitious fifth-generation project as explained in Edward A. Feigenbaum and Pamela McCorduck, *The Fifth Generation: Artificial Intelligence and Japan's Computer Challenge to the World"* (Signet Books, New American Library, 1984).

Conceptual Index

Chapter 3: Winning Frames 37

Most people don't choose frames, they stumble into them. But if you select decision frames carefully, reframe intelligently when you find yourself using an inadequate frame, and match your own frame to the frames of other people you want to influence, you can improve your performance significantly.

Chapter 6: Making the Choice 119

Hundreds of studies have led to an important conclusion about making choices: you can develop procedures that will make your decisions better than your own unaided intuition. Following sound procedures will give you a better chance of achieving your goals than just making a choice because it "feels right."

Our natural biases make learning much more difficult than we realize. When events come out well, we tend to see the success as a result of our own genius. But when events turn out badly, we rationalize—creating an explanation that preserves our positive self-image (but prevents learning). In addition to these biases produced by our desires, we suffer from hindsight effects caused largely by the way our minds work.

Chapter 9: Improving Feedback   189

Most people need not only to understand their own biases, but also to improve the quality of the evidence they receive. They need to recognize inadequate feedback and augment it through better record-keeping and experiments. They also must understand how to learn by studying the processes by which they've made their decisions.

Chapter 10: Changing Your Way of Deciding   211

In a decision audit, you can analyze your own decision-making to identify a few key steps you should take to dramatically improve your decisions. Once you've located the few crucial errors, you'll find that your decision-making can be improved much more easily.

Most of the information in this book comes from a relatively new discipline called cognitive science—the study of how human minds think about and understand the world. Several important trends suggest that the cognitive approach may be the single most useful management advance of the 1990s.

Subject Index

269

Kitchen spindle. *See* Parable of the Kitchen Spindle

Late bloomers, 193, 257
Lateral thinking, 46, 159
Lawyer, 87, 143, 186, 241
Leadership. *See* Directive leadership
Learning, 112, 168, 231, 255
Learning analysis, 199–201
Learning from experience, 173–223, 256
Learning from feedback, 3, 5, 152, 217
Legal trials, 23, 256
Letter to shareholders, 180
Level of confidence, 78, 96–97, 98–101, 103, 115, 141
See also Confidence and Confidence Range
Linear model, 250, 251, 309
Linear model, objective, 138–41, 142
Linear model, subjective, 129–37, 139, 142, 161, 218, 251
Loan officer, 101–102, 200
See also Loans
Loans, 101–102, 124, 139, 143
See also Credit application
Lottery. *See* Spanish National Lottery

Magazine subscription, 143
Majority rule, 33
Management science, 231, 241
See also Operations research
Manufacturing, 16, 23, 97, 161, 208, 234
Marketing, 19, 23, 60, 185, 247
See also New products

Marketing frame, 19, 24, 49, 233
Mathematical model, xii, 54, 226, 229
Medical diagnosis, 139, 142, 168, 246
See also Physicians
Medicine. *See* Physicians
Metadecision, 2, 5–9, 11, 151, 217, 218, 220, 231
Metalworking firm, 103–104
Metaphor, 1, 20, 29–33, 43, 45, 235
Milestones, 181
Military frame, 30, 35, 42, 47, 236
See also War
Misalignment of frames. *See* Frame alignment
Missing feedback, 190–92, 195, 199, 209, 256
Monday morning quarterback, 111
Money pump, 248
Movie industry, 87
Multiattribute utility analysis, 141–42, 250, 252
Multiple anchors, 91
Multiple frames, 36, 42, 59, 63, 233, 234
Mutual respect, 159–161

Negotiations, 6, 51, 61–63, 89, 127, 237
New products, 6, 182, 195, 209
Noise, 177, 193–95, 199, 206, 209, 257
See also Confused feedback
Non-compensatory rules, 125, 249
Nothing-really-new-problem, 183–87

272

NAME INDEX

277

DECISION TRAPS

280

About the Authors

J. Edward Russo is Professor of Marketing and Behavioral Science at Cornell University's Johnson Graduate School of Management. His academic degrees are in mathematics (B.S.: CalTech), statistics (M.S.: University of Michigan), and psychology (Ph.D.: University of Michigan). Dr. Russo has taught at the University of California (San Diego), Carnegie-Mellon University, and the University of Chicago. He has published numerous articles, and is a frequent lecturer to business audiences both in the United States and abroad. His consulting clients include General Motors, the Federal Trade Commission, and the National Bureau of Standards.

Paul J. H. Schoemaker is Associate Professor of Decision Sciences and Policy in the Graduate School of Business at the University of Chicago. His academic degrees are in physics (B.S.: University of Notre Dame), finance (M.B.A.: Wharton), and decision sciences (Ph.D.: Wharton). Dr. Schoemaker has written several books and numerous academic articles. He has lectured and consulted in various industries, including such companies as IBM, GM, Harris Trust & Savings Bank, T. Rowe Price, Ameritech, McCann-Erickson, and Kidder Peabody & Co. His international clients have included the Thomson Group (England), Shell International (Holland), Domtar (Canada), and Fletcher-Challenge (New Zealand). He is also a director of Decision Strategies International.